Praise for *The New Power Base Selling*

"To be successful in sales, it takes 10 percent inspiration and luck with 90 percent smart work and discipline. *Power Base Selling* has been the most pragmatic and effective guide for many years in my career in professional services. With the new edition, Jim and Ryan are not only sharpening a proven methodology but also adding an essential element in an ever more competitive environment, namely Unexpected Value. This is fundamental to differentiate and defend margins."

—Patrick Nicolet
CEO Infrastructure Services, Member of the Group
Executive Committee, Capgemini

"The New Power Base Selling provides salespeople, sales leaders, and chief executives with the knowledge to make the right investment decisions regarding sales opportunities. The methodologies described in this book take the guesswork out of assessing the quality of your sales pipeline and ultimately enable executives to lead a more intelligent sales engine. Intergraph has long been recognized as a leader in protecting lives and property through its software. After implementing the Holden method, sales excellence also became a core competency of Intergraph in just 24 months."

—Bill Campbell
Senior Vice President, Americas, Intergraph Corporation

"Holden and Kubacki have elevated sales to a scientific process that enables sellers to provide exceptional value to their customers. In my 31 years of selling, this is the first definitive work on how to leverage the intangibles of politics, value, and strategy to boost win rates. It's a master's program in sales superiority!"

—Lou Ebling
Global Account Executive, Oracle

"It's time to retire the 'Glengarry leads' mentality of sales effectiveness and take an objective, academic look at the science of selling. Holden and Kubacki deliver a provocative and thoughtful message that up-levels the sales profession to its rightful place in the corporate value chain."

—Peter Ostrow
Vice President & Research Group Director, Customer Management,
Sales Effectiveness, Aberdeen Group

"The New Power Base Selling presents sales as a management science, analogous to the principles of military special operations and counterterrorism, for developing repeatable strategies to defeat competition. In this latest book from the Fox people, Holden and Kubacki identify the doctrine and practices for leveraging political insight, creating unexpected client value, and formulating highly effective

strategies to quickly achieve relative superiority and obtain a decisive advantage in any sales environment. They have successfully brought Sun Tzu into the twenty-first century!"

—Kevin Nowak
Senior Adviser under contract to the US Department of Energy, Office of Security and Cyber Evaluations

"I've been a Holden disciple for a number of years, having found the processes and insights invaluable in helping me to understand how to win in an increasingly complex and crowded marketplace.

"In their book *The New Power Base Selling*, Jim Holden and Ryan Kubacki build upon their time-tested and revolutionary classic, turning the art of selling into a science. Jim and Ryan demonstrate a repeatable, scalable process that will enable any sales force to increase the value of what they sell by establishing sales superiority. Their book details how to leverage the new dynamics of social media and globalization, as well as how to differentiate in the current economic environment.

"Holden and Kubacki's understanding of sales strategies, along with the proper balance between customer and competitive positioning, provides a must-read and a must-implement for any sales professional.

"*The New Power Base Selling* demystifies the selling environment, helping a salesperson to understand how to balance product, political, cultural, and business concerns to provide Unexpected Value to their clients."

—Woody Sessoms
Senior Vice President, Global Enterprise Theatre, Cisco Systems

"This is a book that I couldn't put down. I was spellbound by the new ideas presented and the concepts of Political Advantage, Value Creation, and Compete Strategy. Sellers must advance from information providers to Customer Advisors, and Holden and Kubacki tell us exactly how to do it using language and examples that are both engaging and compelling. Every organization needs to read *The New Power Base Selling* if they want to outfox the competition. It is beautifully written and information-packed."

—Rosemarie Mitchell
CEO, ABS Associates, Inc.

"Holden and Kubacki unveil the science of selling. They show how sophisticated business development can itself create Unexpected Value for clients, drive loyalty, and produce competitive market share."

—Clark Dean
Corporate real estate consultant

"*The New Power Base Selling* is an invaluable tool for anyone looking to achieve the ultimate competitive advantage. The visible and invisible sales tools drilled down on in this book apply to any industry—politics included—and for any individual facing a competitive battle. The book's insights guided my successful and hugely underdog 2010 campaign for US Congress and continue to assist me in the competitive world of Washington, DC."

—Joe Walsh
Congressman, 8th District of Illinois in the
US House of Representatives

"A must-read for selling in today's economy and hypercompetitive marketplace. *The New Power Base Selling* will help ensure value-driven sales rather than price-driven lower-quality business. Jim and Ryan have created an MBA program for selling where all sales professionals can advance to Stage IV Customer Advisors, providing Unexpected Value to customers while driving up win rates."

—Garth Carter
Vice President, State and Local Government/Education,
CIBER, Inc.

"This update to the original thinking of *Power Base Selling* is required reading for every sales professional, whether early in their careers or experienced executives. The key today is relevance and success in an increasingly competitive and complex selling environment. The transition from a product and relationship orientation to a model of political alignment, Value Creation, and Competitive Differentiation yields more wins, trusted advisor status with customers, and larger commission payouts."

—Geoff Nyheim
Vice President, Cloud Services Sales, Microsoft

"Holden and Kubacki masterfully define the many influence factors that drive sales in today's complex organizations. They know what separates super-salespeople from mere account reps, and after reading this book, so will you."

—Paul Gillin
Author of *The New Influencers, Secrets of Social Media Marketing,*
and *Social Marketing to the Business Customer*

"In 1999, when I was running sales for Sprint, we deployed Holden Power Base Selling and we proceeded to win 13 strategic accounts over the next 13 months. My next opportunity to deploy Holden principles came 10 years later at International Game Technology, and we are back again as a dominant force in the marketplace. Jim Holden and Ryan Kubacki, in *The New Power Base Selling,* have captured the essence of selling strategically and describe how to effectively navigate in our complex and competitive environments. We will continue to add to their accumulating 50,000 deals . . . and counting!"

—Eric Tom
Executive Vice President, North American Sales and Global Service,
International Game Technology

"*The New Power Base Selling* is a must-read for anyone looking to create a Customer Advisor sales organization whereby you are looking to increase your deal size, provide value differentiation, and help your customers solve their business problems. The result is a win-win for your company and your customer—that is true value."

—Dave Furtado
Global Vice President of Sales, Ascom Network Testing

"Although the approach to maximizing selling skills is changing dramatically based on advancements and opportunities in technology, the fundamentals of *Power Base Selling* introduced by Jim Holden more than 20 years ago are still exceedingly relevant. Along with Ryan Kubacki, Jim has updated, modernized, and refreshed the application of understanding politics, creating value, and defeating the competition for this generation of sellers and many to follow. How we access the Fox may be changing, but the dynamics of why sales are made can be enhanced by driving the *Power Base Selling* model across the enterprise."

—Jill Billhorn
Vice President Small Business, CDW Corporation

"A comprehensive A–Z book showing simple, yet powerful, concepts on how selling has changed in today's fast-moving environment. Great not only for salespeople but also for executives to better understand their own sales team and those of competitors."

—Doug Lee
CFO, Peerless Networks

"In my experience, the best salespeople will embrace the ideas, practices, and methodologies outlined in *The New Power Base Selling*. The content of this book is fundamental to the success of the modern sales professional."

—Chris Michalak
Client and Accounts Leader, Aon Hewitt

"This book enables salespeople to develop a Fox-inspired strategy to create a path through the minefields of corporate politics, up the slippery slopes of influence, and into the gilded halls of power. It will help business-to-business (B2B) salespeople outfox their competition and rake in millions of dollars in new sales."

—Gerhard Gschwandtner
Owner, Selling Power

"As an executive coach and trainer for more than 30 years, I see this book as the holy grail of real selling. It outlines what everyone in a Power Base knows and understands. If you face any politics in sales (who doesn't?), you must read this book."

—Bailey Allard
President, Allard Associates, Inc.

"I found *The New Power Base Selling* to be a great enhancement to the previous selling concepts discussed in the original *Power Base Selling* (PBS) version . . . kind of an Advanced PBS or PBS 201 structure. Many of the concepts discuss selling from a customer's point of view, along with the mandate to offer not only product but differentiated and Unexpected Value to your customer. This is essential in today's environment. The continual focus on all aspects of your customer's business—politics, competition, value chain, business environment—are crucial for success. I also love the introduction of using social media as an effective sales tool in the selling process. This is a playbook that I would recommend to any sales organization struggling to compete in today's competitive environment."

—Greg Baur
Director of Sales, Intel Americas

"As an investor in the venture capital/private equity space who focuses on investing in high-growth founder-owned businesses, I spend a significant amount of my time in the process of selling: selling the value-add of our firm to founders when we are trying to win the deal, helping our portfolio companies sell themselves to potential hires, and helping portfolio companies close complicated enterprise sales. Yet business schools typically spend very little time on the topic of selling strategy. With *The New Power Base Selling,* Holden and Kubacki provide an advanced MBA of selling to drive significant enterprise value."

—Brian Shortsleeve
General Catalyst Partners

"For the sales that matter—and every targeted sale matters—this approach provides the safety net to allow you to answer the question 'Have I done everything I can to prepare for this close?' with a resounding 'Yes!' So many companies have focused on cutting costs for so many years that they have forgotten the skills necessary to create value for customers."

—Jim Dyke
Corporate Vice President, Sales and Marketing,
Psychemedics Corporation

"I meet hundreds of entrepreneurs each year, and only a tiny fraction recognizes sales as a science. The start-ups that understand how to sell have a huge advantage when it comes to building a new and successful business."

—Chris Yeh
Angel investor

"I have leveraged this approach across multiple companies and have found that the principles hold true for seasoned sellers, as well as those just starting out. But, independent of experience, the only way for sellers to remain relevant with customers and partners is to demonstrate that they understand their business and politics while providing Unexpected Value. This book provides the road map to succeed across all of these areas."

—**Nancy Stickney**
Vice President of Sales, Hyland Software

"Whether lawyers are involved in developing business, negotiating settlements, arguing a case in court, or simply explaining their billable rates, we are always selling. Before any lawyer signs up for another continuing legal education (CLE) course, before any law student graduates from law school, and before any partner talks to another client, they should read this book!"

—**Jim McCarthy**
Partner, McDonnell Boehnen Hulbert and Berghoff, LLP

"In making a deal, we can easily misunderstand what our customers truly value—at the cost of the contract. Holden International has made a business out of teaching others how not to make that error. *The New Power Base Selling* explains how we can learn the key human elements to deal-making. I found this book understandable and engaging and know that the principles put forth can lead to success."

—**Rear Admiral David R. Oliver Jr. (Ret.)**
Strategic Advisor, EADS North America, and author of
Lead On and *Making It in Washington*

THE NEW
POWER
BASE
SELLING

THE NEW POWER BASE SELLING

Master the Politics, Create Unexpected Value and Higher Margins, and Outsmart the Competition

Jim Holden
Ryan Kubacki

WILEY

John Wiley & Sons, Inc.

Library of Congress Cataloging-in-Publication Data:
Holden, Jim, 1948–
    The New Power Base Selling: Master the Politics, Create Unexpected Value and Higher Margins, and Outsmart the Competition / Jim Holden, Ryan Kubacki.
        p. cm.
    Rev. ed. of: Power Base Selling. ©1990.
    Includes index.
    ISBN: 978-1-118-20667-6 (hardback); ISBN: 978-1-118-22862-3 (ebk)
    ISBN: 978-1-118-24094-6 (ebk); ISBN: 978-1-118-26583-3 (ebk)
        1. Sales personnel.   2. Sales management.   3. Selling.   4. Competition.
    I. Kubacki, Ryan, 1973–   II. Holden, Jim, 1948– Power Base Selling.   III. Title.
HF5439.5.H65   2012
658.85—dc23

                                                                        2012003557

Printed in the United States of America
10 9 8 7 6 5 4 3 2 1

This book is dedicated to the executives, sales managers, and sellers who are leading the charge in transitioning sales to that of a management science, one that can be defined, understood, and measured. As such, the days of viewing sales as an art—a way of explaining what has not been understood—are coming to an end. This means:

- The elevation of the sales profession
- The ability to dramatically accelerate the development of sellers
- Enhanced hiring of sellers with defined and measurable sales competencies
- Stronger sales management coaching
- The true ability to align Sales with Marketing, Human Resources (HR), and Finance

All of this means higher win rates, with better margins and higher customer satisfaction, particularly at the customer executive levels. It is our hope that this book, along with the help of these progressive sellers, managers, and executives, will create definitive change in moving sales to a management science—literally becoming an inflection point in the sales profession.

But our dedication doesn't stop there. In the world of competition, there is no more intense competitive environment than that of military operations. This is an area where the transition to that of a management science has been critical, particularly in Special Operations, where a small force takes on a much larger, often better-equipped, enemy force. Drawing corollaries from this domain to sales has been very helpful in our management science efforts. In that process, we continue to develop a deeper and even more profound appreciation for the remarkable men and women of our military who put themselves in harm's way to protect the freedom and liberty of our nation.

As an expression of appreciation, Holden International will donate 15 percent of The New Power Base Selling royalties to the Wounded Warrior Project.

CONTENTS

Chapter 14
Appear where you are not expected.

Chapter 15
If the enemy's forces are united, separate them.

Chapter 16
Though the enemy be stronger in numbers, we may prevent him from fighting.

Epilogue
Lead me, follow me, or get out of my way.

FOREWORD

The nature of sales has changed dramatically since the hugely successful *Power Base Selling: Secrets of an Ivy League Street Fighter* first appeared in 1990. The era of Internet-powered globalization, along with a recent recession, has made buyers more discerning and demanding than ever.

And yet, the fundamentals still apply. Large-scale corporate sales still require preparation, persistence, and a deep understanding of the customer. And they still involve real human beings, with all their brilliance and flaws.

In *The New Power Base Selling,* the sales world now has an updated guide that takes into account the timeless realities of human nature—as well as the contemporary tools that can empower a sales team to capitalize on that nature.

Through their hands-on research into thousands of sellers and competitive deals, Jim Holden and Ryan Kubacki demonstrate the importance of mastering the intangibles: the internal politics and individual motivations that invisibly—and inevitably—shape every transaction.

At a time when products and services are often at relative parity, these intangibles can be the primary differentiator in the success of a sale. But mastering them requires more than simple alertness; it requires a discipline that borders on the scientific.

In that regard, *The New Power Base Selling* represents an important advance for the profession of selling. It applies logic and metrics to the complex relationships that determine the outcome of a considered purchase. Then it goes where its predecessor couldn't go, by demonstrating how to harness social media and other online resources to gather intelligence on both buyers and competitors.

These lessons are especially relevant within the ever-changing software industry, where today's influencer is tomorrow's authority. But they apply to any industry in which the key to success is not only knowing one's customer but also deeply understanding that customer's business value, political value, and cultural value.

Through its unique perspectives and practical techniques, *The New Power Base Selling* will take its place on the required reading list at my company, SAP. I expect it will at yours, too.

May the best Stage IV Customer Advisors win!

—Bill McDermott
Co-CEO
Member of the Executive Board
SAP AG
Newtown Square, Pennsylvania

ACKNOWLEDGMENTS

JIM HOLDEN

At the genesis of this new book project we knew that it would become the core of our firm's marketing efforts, but what we did not recognize was that it would soon become the epicenter of the firm and all that it stands for in helping sellers become more successful. And behind all of that and everything that has gone before it, taking us to where we are today, stands one person who has been my strength and inspiration for the past 38 years: my wife and Chief Financial Officer (CFO) of the firm, Chris Dalghren Holden. Without her, this book would not have been possible!

RYAN KUBACKI

First, I would like to thank Jim and Chris Holden for their generous mentorship and loving friendship. Working on this project under Jim's coaching has been among the most profound experiences of my life. I am grateful. Second, I am proud to work with our team at Holden International, whose talent and dedication apply this important research to improve our clients' businesses every day. In particular, Matt Martin and Paul Dillon made valuable contributions to this book. Most important, thank you to my wife and Marketing Director of our firm, Jana Meader Kubacki. Her contributions in research, data analysis, and editing deepened the insight and accelerated the availability of this project. More significantly, her love, friendship, and sense of humor make our life journey meaningful, exciting, and fun.

PART 1

SALES AS A MANAGEMENT SCIENCE

CHAPTER 1

SEEING THE INVISIBLE

It is not the strongest of the species that survives, nor the most intelligent, but the one most responsive to change.

—often attributed to Charles Darwin

"Know this about yourself: there is only one reason professional salespeople lose orders. They are OUTSOLD," began our first book, *Power Base Selling,* in 1990. Assessing over 28,000 sellers and coaching more than 50,000 competitive deals since then affirms that the best sellers are politically astute, driven to provide significant value to customers, and strategically competitive, as a matter of habit.

The best sellers win because *how* they sell increases the value of *what* they sell. In fact, how they sell adds value for their customers and for their own company, beyond the value inherent in their company's product, price, and brand, as shown in Figure 1.1. Even without product superiority or price parity, the best sellers outsell their competition *and* please their customers. They are a source of competitive advantage for their company and are compensated accordingly. And you can be, too!

Most sellers do not gain clarity about their customers' informal political structure—*the Power Base*—that really makes an organization run. At the same time, they focus on *only* their customer and do not *engage their competition.* Without insight into politics and competitors, it is almost impossible to get a sense of the larger issues that will determine your ability to improve your customer's business, deepen loyalty, and win deals.

Let's look at a practical example. Meet Amy. She was selling an online software solution to a large retail customer. When she previously sold to this customer, the Information Technology (IT) team made most of the decisions. In this current sales situation, she believed that she would close the deal because the IT team had confirmed that her product was the most innovative, it best matched their buying criteria, and she knew the

3

Figure 1.1
Maximizing Sources of Competitive Advantage

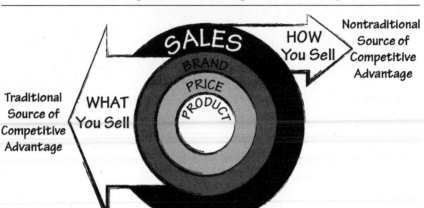

IT organization chart inside and out. The Chief Information Officer (CIO), with whom she had met, appeared to be supportive. In addition, she linked her product's value to business impact for the customer. Specifically, she made the case to the IT Department that her solution would facilitate more efficient communication among the customer's supply chain. This, in turn, would enable her customer to stock lower-priced products on its store shelves much faster. Amy correctly identified this as an important business issue for the customer during a prolonged economic slowdown.

Confidently, Amy informed her manager of the probable win and began to think about how she would spend her commission check. Then, something started not to feel right. The customer had not given her the official order, and her contacts in the IT Department were not returning her emails or calls. After several weeks, the customer informed her that they "went in a different direction." Amy was caught off guard. Her product was the best in the market. She established business value and developed a good relationship with the customer, who made it clear that things were looking good for her. She dreaded telling her manager, who had already forecasted the business as a win to upper management.

Have you ever been in Amy's shoes? What happened? What didn't she see? To find out, let's meet Sara, who is the Account Manager for Amy's competitor, calling on the same customer. Like Amy, Sara sells for a technology company and met with the customer's IT team. Sara also positioned the business value of getting lower-priced products on the customer's shelves quicker. However, *Sara saw three things that Amy did not.*

1. **Sara studied the politics of the customer organization, seeing how authority *and influence* flowed.** She identified that there had recently been management changes at the customer organization. An IT governance committee had been created to evaluate all IT decisions. This group consisted of company leaders from the Business, Finance, and Legal Departments. Sara recognized that this was something new. A *new type of Power Base* had formed. Its influence would likely assert itself over the IT team's authority. Sara utilized social media sites such as LinkedIn and Facebook to gain as much insight as she could on the new players and identified patterns and connections in their past. She met with several of them and asked thoughtful questions, made observations, and tried to confirm hypotheses she had formed regarding the new flow of influence.

   While listening to the customer's quarterly earnings call, Sara became aware that the customer's Chief Financial Officer (CFO) had launched a new initiative, called Supply Chain Leadership, that focused on building relationships with more financially stable suppliers to reduce costly and disruptive supplier turnover. Sara also knew that the customer's Chief Legal Counsel was focused on data privacy issues.

   Furthermore, through the course of her meetings, Sara observed that political conflict was taking place between the customer CIO and CFO. The CFO wanted IT to be more accountable to company initiatives, while the CIO sought independence. Sara noticed that the CIO's influence seemed to be waning among his own team, while the CFO was a proven company leader.

2. **Sara provided the customer with Unexpected Value in addition to meeting the customer's stated needs.** Working with an IT Director, Sara produced a quantified expression of value that reflected a product solution that was 90 percent as capable as the alternative. Still, this solution represented *expected value* to the customer. Sara needed more. To provide *unexpected customer value,* not only did she stress compliance with the new initiative, but, focusing on the financial strength of her company, she also stressed the clear data privacy policies that the CFO could announce as an early example of his new initiative.

3. **Sara assessed her competition and formulated a sales strategy.** She analyzed who Amy was calling in the account and what type of value Amy was proposing. After firsthand evaluation, Sara concluded that the product Amy was proposing had superior capability. However,

Amy's company's unclear financial health and unproven data privacy policies represented potential vulnerability.

Armed with her political and competitive insight, Sara formulated a sales strategy and partnered with an IT Director to approach the CFO, shifting the decision focus from *only* the stated buying criteria defined by the IT Department to *also include* the ability to fulfill the broader organizational needs as defined by the CFO and Chief Legal Counsel.

At the end of the day, Sara outsold Amy and better served her customer by seeing the three intangibles: politics, Unexpected Value, and strategy.

SELLING SKILLS ARE NOT ENOUGH

It's fairly common knowledge that you must master certain skills to succeed in sales. Abilities such as prospecting, asking good questions, structuring a sales call, building a business case for your product, and establishing rapport with a customer, to name just a few, are essential. However, a majority of the techniques that dominate today's notion of selling help sellers in only one dimension of their efforts: establishing the relationship between seller and buyer. Focusing solely on a prospective buyer assumes that there is only one thing between you and getting the order—the customer. It produces a distorted vision of what selling is all about, and it blinds you to the real threat—the competition.

Think about it this way: as much as you want the customer's business, so does someone else. But typical sales campaigns don't make provisions for competitive threats. Amy's "quote and hope" mentality will not be enough when she's up against an advanced seller like Sara. She needs a more complete sales approach, one that incorporates a view of the world as it really is—a three-dimensional interplay between you, your customer, and the competition, as shown in Figure 1.2.

Figure 1.2
Selling Is Multi-Dimensional

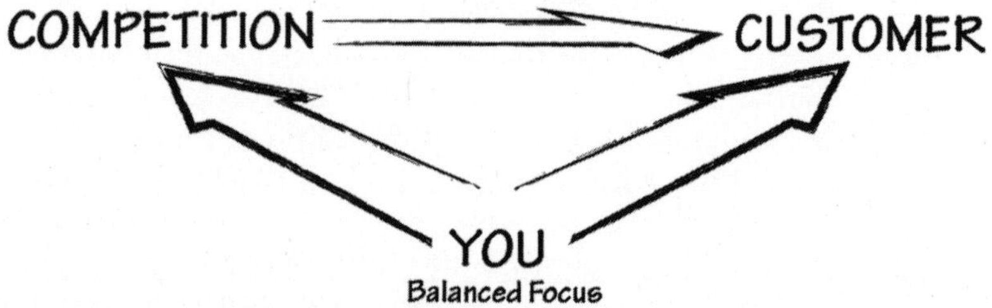

COMPETITION ————————⟶ CUSTOMER

YOU

Balanced Focus

GOOD PRODUCTS ARE NOT ENOUGH

Without question, a superior product, price, and brand give you an advantage. However, the times when you have an exceptional product and are the only game in town are rare; and although you can coast along for a while on only the capabilities and reputation of what you offer, this won't last long. These glad circumstances mislead many people into believing they are selling well—when in reality, the product is doing all the work. The seller is just along for the ride.

This is far more serious than a mere case of mistaken identity. If you judge yourself and your efforts by the strength of your product, you might also judge the potency of your competitors only by the strength of their products—and make a fatal error in the process because:

The best product does not always win.

As much as product superiority can produce competitive advantage, it can also lull you into a false sense of security, as Amy found out.

A lot of sellers do not sell; they surf. Their prospecting is more like searching for the perfect wave than working to make things happen in accounts. They do not create demand. They become adept only at servicing demand, identifying niches for "hot" products that have developed a certain momentum and appeal. As with champion surfers, they make the job look easy—and it may be easy, for a while, until the currents shift. And they always do.

THE RELEVANCE REVOLUTION

It is hard to imagine a time when more currents have shifted than from 1998 to the present. New skills, attitudes, behaviors, mind-sets, and approaches are now required for sellers to thrive. However, insight from our seller surveys and deal reviews indicate that sellers are struggling to keep up with a business market that has been changed forever.

We see five trends disrupting traditional selling methods and challenging seller relevance, as shown in Figure 1.3.

1. *Online distribution models do not require human sellers.* The rise of the Internet and the advances of computing have made it possible for buyers to purchase products with less direct interaction with sellers. Business-to-consumer online sales models, such as Amazon.com, are now finding their way into business-to-business sales. Industry analysts speculate that over time, customers will manage many of their

Figure 1.3
Disruptive Trends

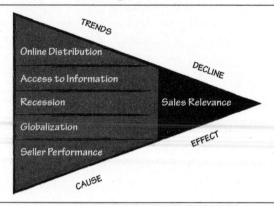

supplier relationships with little or no interaction with sellers. This has prompted Gerhard Gschwandtner, Chief Executive Officer (CEO) of *Selling Power,* to ask in a recent editorial, How many salespeople will be left by 2020?[1] "If we don't find and fill a need faster than a computer, we won't be needed," he concludes.

2. *Access to information has increased buyer leverage.* Pre-Internet, customers had to meet with the seller to learn about the product. Sellers could define their relevance by their mere presence, as an information provider. Now, most customers are well informed about products, having studied websites, participated in online demos, and attended webinars. Therefore, a customer who meets with a seller expects more than product information.

3. *The Great Economic Recession has increased buyer scrutiny and complexity.* The economic challenges that started in 2008 have forced all companies to insist on stronger business justification for all expenses. The result has been an increased number of customer individuals involved in the buying process. Gone are the days when you could sell to one person or even one department, as Amy found out in our earlier example. Now, there are buying committees and professional procurement departments to navigate.

4. *Globalization has increased competitive intensity.* Better access to education and the increased wealth of nations has increased the number

---

[1] Gerhard Gschwandtner, *Selling Power* editorial, May/June 2011.

and intensity of qualified competitors from more educated countries. The rise of China, India, Russia, and Brazil, to name just a few,
is changing the face of global competition. Further intensifying this
competition is the difficulty of sustaining product superiority in a
world where the Internet and other computing advances have lev-
eled the playing field by increasing the speed of commoditization.

5. *Seller performance is not meeting company expectations.* Aberdeen Group,
a leader in analyzing sales effectiveness and training, reports that
most sellers are not achieving their sales quotas.[2] They report that
at the "industry average middle 50% of companies" just 49 percent
of sellers achieve their annual quota; at the "laggard bottom 30% of
companies" just 4 percent achieve their quota; and even at the "best
top 20% of companies" only 87 percent achieve their annual quota.
This means that *less than half* of sellers are meeting the expectations
that their companies have for them!

The result is that sellers are in the midst of a Relevance Revolution. From
the customer perspective, a seller must evolve from the role of an information provider who shows up with extensive PowerPoint presentations,
along with an eagerness to conduct product demonstrations, to that of a
Customer Advisor. The latter helps customers improve their businesses and
competitiveness. In the eyes of their own company, sellers are being asked to
help win market share and provide intelligence to enhance the company's
overall competitive advantage—to help them grow during challenging economic times.

The implications for sellers are real:

**There is a slippery slope from being outsold to being
OUTPLACED.**

To succeed in this new market, the best sellers are no longer relying on
traditional advantages inherent in their company's product, price, and brand.
They seek more than a "quote and hope" approach. The best sellers are
elevating their profession by becoming *nontraditional* sources of competitive
advantage. How? By understanding sales as a management science, particularly as it relates to employing sales strategy.

---

[2]Sales Training 2011: Uncovering How the Best-in-Class Sustain, Reinforce, and Leverage
Best Selling Practices, Peter Ostrow, Research Director, Aberdeen Group, September 2011.
For the full report, visit www.aberdeen.com.

SEEING THE ROAD FORWARD TO SUCCESS

Sales strategy consists of identifying how you will achieve relative superiority—that is, the point at which you have a decisive advantage over your competition.[3] In other words, strategy answers the question, "What are you counting on to win?" And winning means improving your customers' businesses and growing your company's revenue and profits by defeating a competitor trying to do the same thing. Insight from our seller surveys and deal reviews outlines three specific nontraditional sources of relative superiority that advanced sellers both "see" and "manage," while others do not, enabling them to lead the change in this market. More specifically, the best sellers:

1. Start with a focus on customer *politics* by identifying influence and going beyond the tangible authority of organization charts to know who to call on.
2. Provide *unexpected customer value* that goes beyond the stated and expected value associated with a sales opportunity to significantly advance a customer's business, while differentiating themselves from the competition.
3. Formulate a *sales strategy* that leverages the largely invisible elements of influence, unexpected customer value, and sales cycle timing, along with Competitive Differentiation and vulnerability, to build on the more traditional sources of competitive advantage and decisively win business.

This book presents how to see and manage these three invisible intangibles—politics, Unexpected Value, and strategy—and have them work together in an interconnected way to achieve relative superiority and maximize value to your customers and your company (see Figure 1.4). Simply put:

We present the way to win by seeing sales as a management science.

---

[3] Relative superiority is defined by William H. McRaven in his book *Spec Ops* (Novato, CA: Presidio Press, 1995).

Figure 1.4
Nontraditional Sources of Relative Superiority—The Three Intangibles

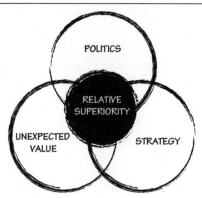

Our journey continues in Chapter 2, where we outline what great selling looks like when politics, unexpected customer value, and strategy are mastered. We consider this chapter an advanced "MBA of selling" that is practical, relevant, and empirically based. From there we dive deeply into politics, then value, and, finally, you will learn how to package it all together to formulate sales strategy.

As you will see in the next chapter, these three areas will significantly accelerate your development and sales performance in the shortest amount of time possible. Our aim is to assist you in reaching a new level of professional success that is acknowledged by your company, where you are viewed as a valued source of competitive advantage—an asset to be recognized and compensated accordingly.

CHAPTER 2

THE MBA OF SELLING

Learning is like rowing upstream; not to advance is to drop back.
—Chinese Proverb

Sellers who are able to identify strategy to achieve relative superiority in their accounts are a powerful source of competitive advantage. However, most companies or business school elites fail to recognize this—even though sellers are a company's final frontier to customer value and to engage and defeat competition (Figure 2.1).

Figure 2.1
Sales as the Final Frontier

So, why is there this perception that sellers are not, themselves, a source of competitive advantage? Two factors seem to be at play here.

First, selling is intangible in comparison to products, product development, customer support organizations, and so on. Most sellers work offsite at customer locations, out of sight of company management. Sure, executives see sales results, but they usually attribute these results to the value of whatever it is they're selling. Since the world tends to discount the intangible in favor of what can be easily seen, felt, and therefore managed, sellers are frequently undervalued.

Second, high-performing sellers and business developers are often not understood. Management looks at what they do as an art, which strangely provides them with an explanation as to why they don't understand selling for what it truly is: a mix of science, process, and interpersonal ability. This definition explains why only 35 of the 4,495 degree-granting institutions in the United States provide students with the opportunity for a minor or major in sales at the undergraduate level and only eight offer an

MBA with a sales focus.[1] We believe selling is a management science, just like engineering, finance, operations, and marketing. Selling can be documented, measured, and replicated—and therefore, intelligently managed. But this assumes that people understand selling as a management science; providing such understanding is our mission in this chapter.

THE HOLDEN FOUR STAGE MODEL

We initially introduced the Holden Four Stage Model of Sales Proficiency in the first edition of *Power Base Selling* years ago. We have refined and tested the model repeatedly since that time, developing it into an industry standard for defining and measuring sales effectiveness. We use it here to present the building blocks that enable sellers to formulate strategy to achieve relative superiority in accounts. The model shows how this type of advanced selling is a management science—one that can be understood, managed, scaled, and optimized to drive maximum revenue.

The Holden Four Stage Model shows that the best sellers do something that most sellers do not. They manage, well and in balance, both *customer and competitive* issues. These are shown in Figure 2.2. How well sellers manage this balancing act is described in terms of four stages of sales proficiency.

Figure 2.2
The Holden Four Stage Model

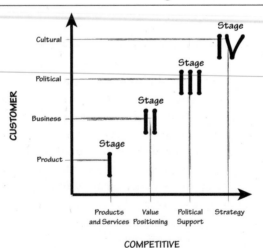

[1] The number 4,495 comes from the Digest of Education Statistics (http://nces.ed.gov/programs/digest/d10/tables/dt10_276.asp); the information about sales majors is from DePaul University Center for Sales Leadership, "Universities and Colleges Sales Education Landscape," 2009, David Hoffmeister, MBA, Executive in Residence.

As we walk through each stage, you will have the ability to assess yourself, your sales manager, and, in fact, your entire sales organization. Perhaps more important, you will develop the ability to describe precisely what you do and why you do it in a language that management can understand. You can have confidence in the fact that the model is based on science and engineering and backed by extensive data that distinguishes it from the traditional thinking so often put forth in sales books and training.

First, great sellers manage customer issues very well. Per the vertical axis in Figure 2.2, they present value to a customer along a continuum, starting with the specific value *their* product provides. Although all sellers address product value, performers go further and connect that value to critical business issues that move them up the Sales Value Chain. Behind these business issues often sit political considerations, such as aligning with powerful people and advancing their organizational interests. The latter is a nontraditional expression of value, which marks the domain of the high performer.

The top of the continuum presents an organizational expression of value. We know that when a seller can generate business value in a manner that supports the customer's principles and beliefs—the factors that characterize that customer's culture—the perception of value is maximized. Conversely, operate in a manner that the customer does not understand or appreciate and the risk that they will discount the value is very high. In short, the *way* in which you create value can be just as important within some accounts as the value itself.

Still, you cannot manage the customer environment in a vacuum. It must be managed in balance with the competitive environment, which is shown on the horizontal axis of the Holden Four Stage Model. This also works on a continuum and first requires that a seller assess the strengths and weaknesses of competitors' products. As sellers then move to the right on the horizontal axis, life gets a bit more interesting. Here they determine how the competition has positioned its value in terms of business impact for the customer, political impact as it relates to powerful customer individuals, and organizational impact on the company. Moreover, they look at how the competition will likely capitalize on these expressions of value in terms of strategy.

Sales performers do many things well. However, as we introduced in Chapter 1, perhaps their most distinctive attribute is their ability to *clearly identify* what they are counting on to win. *Strategy* is their intellectual sword, but they're also aware that possessing insight into the competition's strategy is just as important as having one of their own. Only then can a seller feel confident that what he or she is doing during a sales campaign is directionally correct—and that it will lead to victory.

Managing the customer and competitive environments in balance gives us the ability to characterize sales proficiency in terms of four stages. You will see patterns materialize that help us label each stage as follows:

Stage I: Emerging Sellers
Stage II: Solution Sellers
Stage III: Compete Sellers
Stage IV: Customer Advisors

FOUR STAGES OF SALES PROFICIENCY

The Holden Four Stage Model brings great selling to life by examining it through five dimensions:

1. Intent
2. Focus
3. Relationship
4. Value
5. Knowledge

Intent

In terms of *intent,* Stage I Emerging Sellers want simply to be considered. Making the short list is cause for celebration; they merely want to survive today and grow into the job. Think about when you might have been at this point in your career. Stage II Solution Sellers differ in that they want to make a sale. In fact, many of these individuals would sacrifice longer-term customer loyalty in favor of a short-term revenue win, particularly at the end of the quarter, when the pressure to close orders becomes intense. Each sales situation is the main event for these sellers. However, they often lack an objective and quantitative approach to determining whether they should pursue an opportunity. They essentially go after anyone—or anything—that's warm and breathing.

Stage III Compete Sellers want to "own" the customer department where purchases are being made. They place the emphasis on repeat sales and work to develop a long runway of business. In contrast to Stage II Solution Sellers, they use written criteria to answer the following questions:

• Should I pursue this business?
• Can I win this business?
• Will winning lead to *more* business?

Stage IV Customer Advisors carry the thinking even further. They want to "own" the *account,* seeking the lion's share of the business. These people not only service demand but know how to create it in a politically astute manner. Customer Advisors work hard to establish themselves as thought leaders with their customers, often providing Unexpected Value that earns them insider status. They don't just take business; they make sensible business recommendations that reflect out-of-the-box thinking. And when they need to tell a customer something that they know the customer might not want to hear but needs to hear, they diplomatically explain their position.

Perhaps the customer is about to embark on a new initiative that the Customer Advisor knows from experience will fail. Instead of remaining silent—which so many sellers would do to avoid confronting or disagreeing with the customer—the Customer Advisor might say, "I know that you are very excited about this project and we want to be supportive, but our experience in this area suggests that there could be significant risk of failure. Can we take a few minutes to discuss this?"

Take a look at Figure 2.3 regarding sales *intent*. At what stage would you objectively place yourself? Where would you place your sales organization?

Figure 2.3
Holden's Four Stages of Sales Proficiency: Intent

	Stage I Emerging Seller	Stage II Solution Seller	Stage III Compete Seller	Stage IV Customer Advisor
INTENT	To Be Considered	To Make a Sale	Repeat Business	Insider Status

Focus

The second dimension is *focus*. It's a given that all sellers address product issues. However, Stage I Emerging Sellers center most of their time and effort on the *product*. They have been trained on product strengths and weaknesses and tend to view the world in this context. Stage II Solution Sellers have learned that effective selling also requires them to look at the product through the customer's eyes, which is their primary focus. They're aware that they must recognize and address customer needs with empathy, compassion, and commitment. To their credit, these Solution Sellers focus on the customer with an eye toward coming up with solutions in order to get closer to the real needs driving the sales situation. As an example, Stage II Solution Sellers will often put just as much time into making a solution work for the customer as they did in selling that solution.

Stage III Compete Sellers certainly do not lose sight of the product and customer; however, they concentrate primarily on the *competition* and determining what it will take to win. The competition is at the top of their list, earning them the title of Compete Sellers. Whereas other sellers tend to avoid the opposition, this group actively seeks competitive intelligence— that is, information from many sources, including other sellers within the supplier company who have competed with a specific competitor—in an attempt to figure out what they can expect from the competitor. They then formulate a strategy to win the business that takes this competitive information into account.

You can see an example of this when one supplier is in the lead. That supplier understands what the customer needs, has created an effective solution distinct from the competitor's, and has aligned with powerful people within the account. At the same time, any competitive activity could suggest that the competitor might attempt to change the buying criteria in the 11th hour of the sales situation, just as it is peaking. Not knowing how this might happen—but being aware that it has occurred in the past—the Stage III Compete Seller works to collapse the time frame by providing the customer with an incentive to place the order sooner. This enables him or her to preempt the competition and win the business.

Stage IV Customer Advisors go even further. They look beyond the product, customer, and competition to center in on the *customer's customer* and their competition. They determine how their company will contribute to the customer's business success over time by providing significant Unexpected Value. As such, solutions are tied to customer-critical business issues that move them up the Sales Value Chain where there is strong Competitive Differentiation—and where elasticity of demand will support higher pricing that corresponds with the increased value. These sellers work to conceptually draw a line from their solutions to increases or decreases in the customer's market share.

An example might be introducing check imaging to a community bank in order to free employees up from mundane tasks to focus on better customer support and service. Whereas other sellers would perhaps stress the cost savings of reduced labor content, the Customer Advisor puts an equal emphasis on the ability to pursue higher-value activities that are aligned with strategic company initiatives, such as increasing customer satisfaction.

Regarding *focus,* look at Figure 2.4. At what stage would you objectively place yourself? Where would you place your sales organization?

Figure 2.4
Holden's Four Stages of Sales Proficiency: Focus

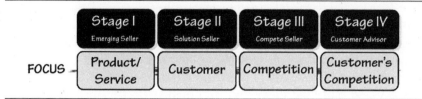

Relationship

That brings us to the third dimension: *relationship.* For the Stage I Emerging Seller, the word *relationship* is a misnomer, as the tendency to focus on product renders interaction with the customer casual at best. Stage II Solution Sellers start to build trust, because they recognize that they are selling solutions, which inherently contain intangible components such as service, support, and responsiveness to problems. As such, it is imperative that the customer trust the seller and that the seller propose a viable solution.

Stage III marks the beginning of a real relationship—one that can weather a storm if something goes wrong. It is based on mutualism that is based on common trust, respect, and value. Stage III Compete Sellers build a bridge between supplier and customer based on what both consider valuable. And this doesn't refer just to business and product value; it also accounts for political value, where key individuals can advance their agendas in balance with the business value each company receives.

An example of this kind of mutually beneficial relationship that exists in nature is that between the rhinoceros and the tickbird. The tickbird eats the ticks found on the rhino, getting a free lunch, if you believe in such a thing, and the rhino frees himself of those pesky bugs. Sometimes, the birds will even hop down onto the mud to catch a fleeing tick and perhaps get stepped on by the unaware rhino. But, no problem; another bird simply flies in. And that is the vulnerability of even a Stage III Compete Seller—he or she can be quickly replaced.

The fate of Stage IV Customer Advisors is less tenuous, because the relationship is symbiotic at this point; the two companies depend on each other and often share a common set of values that produce a degree of cultural fit. Since it would be difficult and costly for either to disengage, the organizations are bridged together at the highest possible level. An example of this has been the strong Microsoft and Intel "Wintel" relationship that for many years has defined the personal computing industry.

A sales example is the situation in which a customer wants to purchase a particular solution from you that you truly know is not right for that company. Perhaps the solution is based on technology that the supplier company will soon be selling off or not supporting in the future. Many sellers would simply take the business; however, a Customer Advisor would not if there was any doubt that his or her solution might not be in the best interest of the customer. Customer Advisors take both the long view, with repeat business in mind, and hold themselves to a higher standard than most sellers when it comes to the value they provide customers.

Regarding *relationship,* look at Figure 2.5. At what stage would you objectively place yourself? Where would you place your sales organization?

Figure 2.5
Holden's Four Stages of Sales Proficiency: Relationship

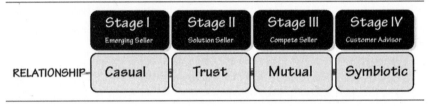

Value

The fourth behavior centers on *value.* Customers see Stage I Emerging Sellers as individuals who provide product options and information. As discussed earlier, this has largely been replaced by the Internet research that customers do before contacting a seller. Stage II Solution Sellers, on the other hand, have adopted a solutions approach to selling that centers on the operational aspects of what the customer is trying to accomplish while also focusing on the business value that it represents.

Stage III Compete Sellers understand that business value is clearly important. However, they also know that they will likely not drive repeat business if they do not clearly express what political contribution they're making as well. A contribution like this occurs when Compete Sellers professionally and ethically participate in the healthy and natural Power Struggles for resources, as an example, or work to advance the aspirations of powerful people within an organization. All these actions are completed in an attempt to maximize what is in the best interest of the customer organization in order to drive long-term business.

An example of this occurs when a salesperson is competing for a repeat order to service the need for more customer capacity at the same time that a key decision maker has just been replaced by a new individual. The Compete Seller knows that this could be a problem. If the new guy has a bias for a competitor whose equipment is compatible with the existing systems, a switch could be made. Quickly spending time with the new player allows the Compete Seller to understand whether recognition and vertical mobility are important to him. As a result, the Compete Seller may alter her proposal to provide additional value beyond just meeting the capacity requirement. Although it's not a lot, it could be sufficient for the new decision maker to put his stamp on the approach. After all, politically speaking, there is no recognition in going with a "me too" solution.

Stage IV Customer Advisors aspire to provide value at all levels. They provide a continuum of value that ranges from a specific solution to the political advancement of key customer individuals to operating in a manner that complies with and possibly strengthens the customer's culture—all with the purpose of contributing to their strategic direction. It is this type of selling that allows suppliers to price assertively and have access to long-range customer business information, which in turn impacts forecast quality and builds competitive immunity within accounts. You can see an example of this when a Customer Advisor is able to personify a company's work ethic. He or she places more of an emphasis on understanding the values that the customer considers to be a vital part of how his or her company does business, rather than merely focusing on formulating a good solution. The Customer Advisor then actively incorporates those values into the implementation of the solution.

Let's say that the customer highly values the concept of collaboration. The supplier could have installed a given solution on a turnkey basis without customer involvement but instead forms a working team of both supplier and customer individuals that will, at the end of the day, help the customer better utilize and maintain the equipment. This increases perceptible value because it reflects what is important to the customer.

Regarding *value*, look at Figure 2.6. At which stage would you objectively place yourself? Where would you place your sales organization?

Figure 2.6
Holden's Four Stages of Sales Proficiency: Value

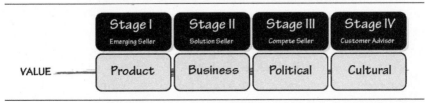

	Stage I	Stage II	Stage III	Stage IV
	Emerging Seller	Solution Seller	Compete Seller	Customer Advisor
VALUE	Product	Business	Political	Cultural

Knowledge

The fifth and final dimension is *knowledge*. Stage I Emerging Sellers spend most of their time amassing large quantities of *data,* which consist of specific facts and figures, for example, a long list of customer executive names. Today's online world has no shortage of data. Websites, blogs, social media sites such as LinkedIn, and Customer Relationship Management (CRM) systems all contain millions and millions of data points.

Stage II Solution Sellers differ in that they are able to turn data into *information,* which is data with a purpose. For example, a customer organization chart takes the data from the list of executive names and places it into a structure that conveys the level of authority of each person, along with who reports to whom.

Stage III Compete Sellers have the ability to rapidly derive significant value from the right information to produce *insight.* An example of this would be to combine the organizational chart with other information to determine the degree of influence that certain individuals have, independent of authority. This provides sellers with insight into the people on whom they should be calling within the account.

The most advanced Stage IV Customer Advisors have the rare ability to discern what information is important to developing insight, as well as how they can effectively use and apply that insight. This is *wisdom.* For example, once the wise seller has identified a powerful customer individual, he or she will politically align with that person to fuel a competitive strategy. In fact, by doing so, it is sometimes possible to even determine how the competition will most likely respond to the strategy. As such, insight—and the application of wisdom to insight—almost always leads to *enhanced* insight, which, in this example, is predictive in nature. Directionally predicting the future is the most powerful manifestation of insight.

It is critical to gather information that allows us to develop insight—particularly nontraditional insight that is counterintuitive for most people. The 80/20 rule applies here; that is, 20 percent or less of all information we could gather on an account is essential to developing important insights. The problem is that most people aren't able to determine *which* 20 percent subset of information is important. As a result, we see many CRM systems and traditional account plans focus on *all* available information. This approach is born out of ignorance, as people are not able to identify key information and, therefore, want the seller to collect all known information.

Regarding *knowledge,* look at Figure 2.7. At which stage would you objectively place yourself? Where would you place your sales organization?

Figure 2.7
Holden's Four Stages of Sales Proficiency: Knowledge

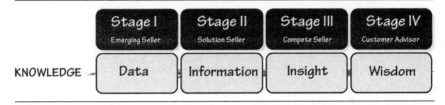

	Stage I Emerging Seller	Stage II Solution Seller	Stage III Compete Seller	Stage IV Customer Advisor
KNOWLEDGE	Data	Information	Insight	Wisdom

Being able to honestly assess where you are in this process is the first step toward improvement. As such, we invite you to complete the full survey. Simply visit www.holdenintl.com and follow the directions. It will take only about 20 minutes, and you'll receive the confidential results immediately.

In addition, being able to make an informed evaluation of your company's entire sales organization can begin to explain why it tends to operate as it does. This could produce an insightful awareness for your management team, while also helping to educate them on what selling really is: a management science. Figure 2.8 provides a summary view.

Figure 2.8
Holden's Four Stages of Sales Proficiency: Expanded

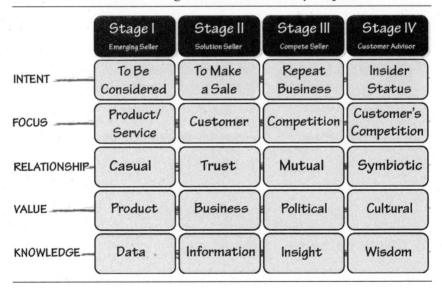

	Stage I Emerging Seller	Stage II Solution Seller	Stage III Compete Seller	Stage IV Customer Advisor
INTENT	To Be Considered	To Make a Sale	Repeat Business	Insider Status
FOCUS	Product/ Service	Customer	Competition	Customer's Competition
RELATIONSHIP	Casual	Trust	Mutual	Symbiotic
VALUE	Product	Business	Political	Cultural
KNOWLEDGE	Data	Information	Insight	Wisdom

PROGRESSING TO HIGHER STAGES

So now that you know where you stand individually, how do you compare with the industry averages? Let's dive into the survey results to find out.

We surveyed 28,463 business-to-business sellers from 35 countries in the years 1998 through 2011. Each seller completed an 80-question online self-assessment in preparation for a Holden sales training program that allowed sellers to see where they placed on the Holden Four Stage Model as they prepared for the rigorous program. We informed each participant that individual results are strictly confidential to ensure honesty and integrity and that we report findings anonymously and on aggregate.

This global study featured 62 percent of companies and 68 percent of sellers residing in the United States and 38 percent of companies and 32 percent of sellers residing outside the United States. The sellers represented 313 different companies of all sizes. Most of the companies were large; 59 percent had annual revenue greater than $1 billion, and 42 percent had annual revenue that exceeded $5 billion. The companies are generally well known, respected in their industries, and operate globally. The survey represented a wide range of industries, with the largest sampling being from the information technology, business services, manufacturing, telecommunications, and financial services areas. Only three companies constituted more than 5 percent each of the total surveys, and the study was completed over multiple years so as not to unduly influence any single-year data findings.

The survey probed for behavioral drivers behind the Holden Four Stage Model by assessing seven core competencies, as shown in Figure 2.9.

Figure 2.9
Sales Competencies

COMPETENCY	THE ABILITY TO...
1) Business Acumen	leverage insight of business issues and industry trends
2) Relationship Adeptness	develop and manage interpersonal connections
3) Value Creation	generate enhanced demand for products and/or services
4) Executive Bonding	establish credibility with senior leadership
5) Political Advantage	capitalize on influential forces in an organization
6) Competitive Differentiation	distinguish and effectively communicate advantages
7) Resource Optimization	secure and employ all appropriate resources in the most efficient and effective manner

Figure 2.10 shows the results we found when we plotted all 28,463 sellers collectively onto the Holden Four Stage Model. The findings confirm what we have observed from approximately 50,000 competitive deals on which we advised and from working with thousands of sellers over the past 33 years: Stage III and IV sellers make up 17 percent and 3 percent of the population, respectively. This type of selling is difficult, not because it is hard, but because it is largely counterintuitive, which makes it uncommon. As a result, only 20 percent of sellers are what we think of as rainmakers.

Figure 2.10
Aggregate Data Results Plotted on the Holden Four Stage Model

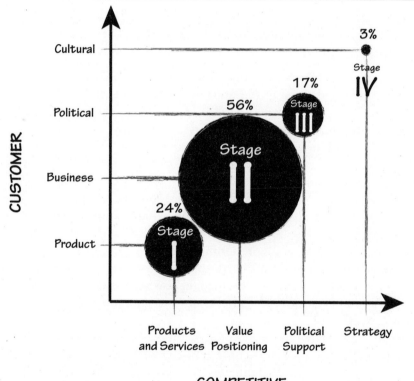

We also discovered that although many sellers progress without much trouble from Stage I to II, they slow down as they move up in Stage II. The data suggest that the progress becomes increasingly more difficult. Often, they misunderstand why selling is getting more difficult and misdiagnose the problem, perhaps by blaming their company. Or, they just settle in as a Stage II Solution Seller and never improve.

Stage II Solution Sellers who develop into Stage III Compete Sellers find that this transition requires that they not only cultivate new skills but also learn an entirely new selling orientation based on unconventional thinking. Stage III and IV selling require that they think geometrically, being able to look at a competitive sales situation from all angles, creating business value, understanding politics, formulating strategy, building executive presence, and more. All these factors create a new orientation for most sellers. And when you superimpose the establishment of this new type of counterintuitive and geometric thinking on top of the need to develop a new set of Stage III and IV skills, you have a real challenge—particularly in a down economy.

Not All Competencies Are Born Equal

When we complement this data with insight from the competitive deals we have coached, three of the seven competencies emerge as most critical. Based on what you know so far, can you guess which ones? They are Political Advantage, Value Creation, and Competitive Differentiation, all nontraditional sources of relative superiority.

Political Advantage provides enhanced access to key business information that is important to Value Creation, in terms of providing customers with Unexpected Value. At the same time, Political Advantage and Value Creation drive Competitive Differentiation because both are nontraditional in nature. In this way, all these elements work as a single, interconnected system in which the sum is greater than the parts.

We also uncovered a fairly surprising fact from our research: it appears that there was little or no improvement in how sellers perceived these three competencies over time—despite the obvious change in the general business market.

Figure 2.11 shows the results of these three competencies. Because sales complexity and number of customer individuals involved in the buying process increased from 1998 through 2011, we expected to see an improvement in Political Advantage during these years, yet there was no substantial improvement. We also anticipated enhanced awareness in the area of Value Creation, given the increased customer scrutiny and need to justify all expenses; however, there was none. Finally, we expected sellers to notice the increase in competitive intensity and, therefore, become more focused on Competitive Differentiation; but once again, the data doesn't show any significant progression. Why might this be?

Figure 2.11
Surprising Data Findings: Little Improvement Over Time

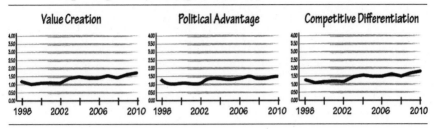

Our data shows us that Political Advantage and Competitive Differentiation are the weakest competencies among the study participants who fell in Stage II, III, or IV. Our hypothesis is that Value Creation, although stronger than the other two competencies, is defined traditionally and therefore underleveraged in moving sellers into Stages III and IV. Companies have done a good job helping sellers to understand, articulate, and deliver traditional value to customers, but this stops short of providing unexpected customer value.

In addition, what has been done has been suboptimized, in terms of sales development and performance, in the absence of the other two competencies, Political Advantage and Competitive Differentiation. Again, the three need to work together. Think of this as a developmental performance strategy, one that we implement in the next chapter with a deep dive into the political reality of influence and authority.

PART 2

POLITICS

CHAPTER 3

INFLUENCE AND AUTHORITY

The secret of my influence has always been that it remained secret.
—Salvador Dali

When coaching the competitive deal reviews, we often heard sellers claim that they would "never get involved in customer politics." But whether they knew it or not—and whether they liked it or not—they already *were* involved in customer politics from the moment they called on the account; they never had a choice. To help improve a customer's business and to win a sale, you have to not only sell people on your ideas but sell the *right* people. So how do you determine who the right people are? The answer lies in understanding customer politics. More specifically, you must gain insight into how the relationship between influence and authority shapes the customer organization's decision-making process. The crucial nature of this realization for sellers lies in the fact that:

Political Advantage is the most important of the nontraditional sources of relative superiority because it fuels the other two: Value Creation and Competitive Differentiation.

In that way, mastering politics is not a choice; it is a requirement. So let's begin by understanding it.

POLITICAL COMPETITION IS HEALTHY

One of the reasons that many people disdain "corporate" politics is because this term brings negative images to mind. *Internal politics* implies that people are competing within an organization, *against one another*—which must be bad. Except that it's not bad. Competition is, in fact, healthy and natural so that a company can prioritize its resources and bring value to its customers. Since customers aren't going to like every idea—and not everything you do will create higher company profits—internal competition ensures that members of your organization vet these ideas appropriately. For example, when launching a new product, it is a healthy dynamic for a company's engineering and marketing teams to debate how the cost of innovation may impact the product's price, and therefore, the customer's elasticity of demand. Success is truly evident only when a company's customers reward or reject the solutions that are a result of these earlier decisions.

Although the fight for personal advancement is an obvious political activity for sellers to observe, it's important to note that people also compete for other, more fundamental reasons. For one, people must vie for influence every day simply to do their jobs. For another, the competition for precious resources is often the most intense, since no company has unlimited assets.

The annual battle of the budget usually requires every department to compete for resources such as money, head count, supplier relationships, executive recognition, and office space. Managers know that they must compete with one another to get good people onto their teams when they're building up staff for a project; and once they build the right staff, they must compete to keep them. As the project gets under way, a variety of interested parties will jockey for position and reach for the reins. Project leaders must constantly contend with one another for control.

All this political competition is so natural that companies are formally organized to create it—and capitalize on it. Managed conflict, or contention management, as it is often called, provokes a separation of powers within an organization. It produces a system of checks and balances and a motivating influence that tends to bring out the best in people—*when* it is well managed. An example of this is the increased rise of cross-functional buying committees, as we saw in the example of Amy and Sara in Chapter 1.

POWER STRUGGLES VERSUS POWER PLAYS

Similarly, we're seeing a new trend emerging that is changing how Information Technology (IT) Departments buy. For the first time ever, business units outside of IT are beginning to dominate what IT purchases. Business needs, such as compatibility of software and hardware to ease IT deployment and maintenance expense, are taking precedence over traditional IT buying considerations. End users are demanding that certain smartphones and tablets become a part of the network—a trend that is likely to continue into the future. Newer technologies such as cloud computing, in which software is delivered as an Internet service rather than a product download, can dramatically reduce software deployment costs. At the same time, these new technologies come with risk, such as the security of confidential information and legal compliance requirements.

In fact, we have seen some cases where cloud sales opportunities are stopped before they ever get off the ground because an in-house attorney has attached liability to a specific cloud-based IT solution. In other situations, however, companies can reach a happy compromise whereby they adopt the cloud concept—but do so behind the company's firewall, as a private nonpublic solution.

As a result, what was once considered a mostly IT sales opportunity has now extended itself beyond this micro-environment to become a business opportunity that's enabled by IT. Today, significant influencers and decision makers who are external to the IT function are casting their will upon the role of IT, changing how customers buy—and therefore how you need to sell and compete for their business.

The absence of such built-in competition would lead to something close to chaos. For example, companies dominated by unchecked Engineering Departments might manufacture products that are never sold. Marketing-driven companies may suffer from fragmented product lines—countless variations of similar products meant to satisfy every possible customer preference that only increase support costs that reduce margins.

Healthy organizations make sure that these two powerful forces keep each other in balance. There may be some intense political battles along the way, but the ongoing competition eventually produces what is best for the company *and* for its customers. Although a written mission statement might spell out a department's focus and responsibilities, the way in which it must interact with other functions cannot easily be specified in such a formal document. There are also no written guidelines about politics for individual employees. People will chart their own path to try to find their way—and it is understood that they will have to contend with the desires of others as they strive for their goals.

Insight from our deal reviews affirms that two types of power conflicts exist: *Power Struggles,* which are healthy, and *Power Plays,* which are parasitic. These are summarized in Figure 3.1.

Figure 3.1
The Anatomy of Power Conflicts

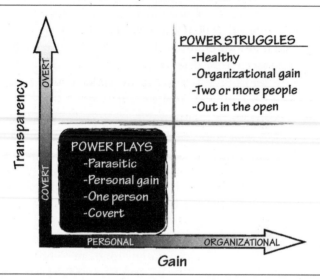

First, there are *Power Struggles*—for example, the dynamic between an unchecked Engineering Department that might manufacture an array of dazzling products that will never find a home and a marketing team whose focus on customer needs could result in too many fragmented product lines. These are healthy, natural competitions for budget, staff, and other resources. They may also reflect a less tangible desire to shape the direction or priorities of an organization. They have the best interest of the company at heart and are conducted in the open.

Power Plays are the opposite of this and are often executed covertly. They are rooted in a desire to enhance personal gain rather than improve organizational value, with power and advancement generally topping the list of motivations. For example, a department manager who makes a play to hire more staff even though the workload or customer demand doesn't warrant it is likely trying to increase head count to elevate his or her perceived importance. Another example is a customer individual who pushes an unqualified, but personally favored, supplier through the evaluation process despite the buying committee's logical objections. The individuals involved in these types of Power Plays may be willing to do anything to impede the career progress of a rival or build up a staff empire to satisfy personal ego.

Great sellers know that it is strategic to get involved in Power Struggles. They also know that if they are on the wrong side, they may end up losing the deal. However, superior and experienced sellers are also careful to never get involved in a Power Play. If you lose a Power Play, you don't just lose the individual deal; you often lose the account as well. And even if you do win, you put your credibility on the line. There is no real upside to getting involved in a Power Play; however, there is significant downside. People who engage in Power Plays often do not survive in the long term. Both colleagues and customers can easily identify their true motivations, and they are forced out as the detrimental cost of their actions on an organization becomes apparent. Before that happens, however, many will suffer by their hand.

Simply put:

Power Struggles are strategic, whereas Power Plays are poison.

Admittedly, it can all feel like part of a game. But it is a good and healthy game, as long as people act professionally and in the best interest of their organization, while improving their own positions. As they do—and as they succeed—an informal political structure begins to form.

THE POLITICAL STRUCTURE

For a business to be organized, it must have a formal structure, that is, a clear distribution of authority and responsibilities. Most organizations go to great effort to clearly communicate this distribution. They want to remove any doubt about people's responsibilities, and as a result, they produce and present an organization chart. Clean lines portray a systematic delegation of authority, responsibilities, and tasks; it depicts the *official* structure.

It is important in selling to understand the official organization chart and to gather insight about the people who are directly involved in a decision. But you won't find out everything you need to know merely by looking at a chart. For example, it does not reveal who will indirectly be involved in the decision. Although these people may not be "official" decision makers, they do *influence* the decision makers. To determine who they are, you need to identify the informal hierarchy—the *political* structure.

An organization's political structure is its *Power Base,* and the people in the Power Base are those who have political strength and *influence.* There is a distinct difference between influence and authority.

Unlike authority, influence is not visible. But the exertion of influence is.

Therefore, unlike the official organization chart, the Power Base generally is not visible. Nobody publishes it for public consumption. And since the Power Base is not easy to see, few sellers do. You have to know what to look for and when to look for it. This is your challenge—and your opportunity. The first mistake many sellers make as they try to get inside an account is to confuse influence with authority. These two are not necessarily synonymous. Authority is found in the formal structure; influence resides in the informal. Many sellers confuse the two because it is certainly possible, even common, for people to exert influence based on their authority. They take what power is formally allocated to them and use it to shape and run the organization. However, it is also possible for some people to exert influence when they do *not* have authority—which they do by virtue of their *association* with authority, by acting "in the name" of someone who has official responsibility.

All sellers come across people who are influential in the buying process but who have no authority. These people may be somewhat junior-level employees, perhaps even in a different department than the one to which you're selling, and their views become central to the buying criteria because the right people value their experience. Or they may be consultants with no authority at all, but they're able to significantly influence decisions based on their association with the managers who hired them.

It is a mistake to assume that those with authority can automatically influence a decision, and it is an equally serious error to believe that people who lack authority have no influence. Figure 3.2 shows how those people who have authority may or may not have influence and how people may have influence despite a lack of authority.

Figure 3.2
The Power Matrix

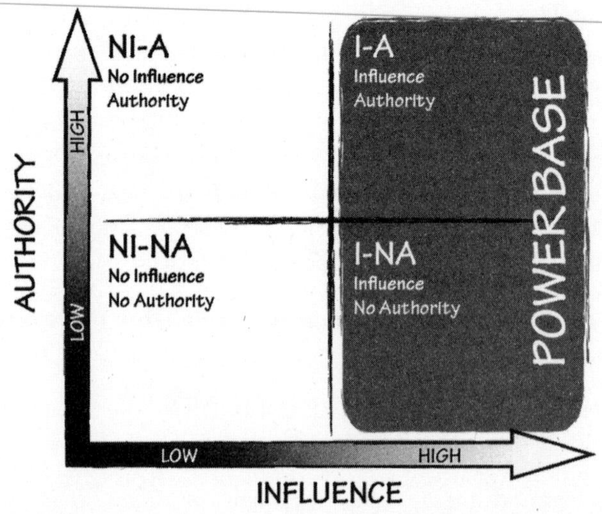

Influence and Authority

The customer individuals who are in the upper right-hand corner of Figure 3.2 are the Influential Authoritarians. They have both authority and influence. They have official responsibility, at or near the top of the organization chart—whether it is that of a company, a division, or a department. They also have political influence because they use their legal power to steer the organization, set its priorities, and establish formal and informal expectations.

Examples of Influential Authoritarians include:

- Chief Executive Officers (CEOs)
- Business unit heads
- Department heads
- Team leaders with responsibility for specific projects

When these leaders issue directives, others enthusiastically and respectfully follow them. Their influence matches their authoritative title.

No Influence, but Authority

The upper left quadrant of Figure 3.2 depicts Non-Influential Authoritarians. These are people who, despite their official titles, do not exert influence in matters of substance for their organizations. For one reason or another, these folks are figureheads who hold their position for some purpose but who do not have a role in the overall actions and passions of the organization. These people may be "empty suits" who are allowed to bide their time until retirement while their companies grow around them. Or they may be individuals who are valued as administrators but not perceived as visionaries who can lead the organization into the future. Others may see them as being excellent at carrying out policy but as contributing little to the creation of policy itself.

Sometimes, these are individuals who have influence, but not in an area that will affect you. Let's assume that you are selling network equipment. A business unit leader may say, "I don't care whose gear we use in the network, as long as it works." While she simply does not want to get involved, that doesn't mean that this individual doesn't have influence in other areas of the business. Always keep in mind that someone who is in the upper left quadrant today might move to the upper right tomorrow if that person deems it appropriate.

As far as sellers are concerned, these are people who may be able to say "no" but who cannot say "yes." For example, if you alienate the head of Procurement, that person may very well have the authority to say "no" or prevent you from advancing. However, with some exceptions, it does not mean that he has the influence to say "yes." Another example of this might occur if a company's Chief Financial Officer (CFO)—or the in-house attorney whom we mentioned earlier—decides to say "no" and uses his organizational authority to stop a buying process.

No Influence, No Authority

It would be ideal if you could always align yourself with Influential Authoritarians. Unfortunately, these people are the most difficult to gain access to in nearly all organizations. So the only alternative for the majority of sellers is to deal with lower-level people in the account. Working at lower levels does have advantages. Typically, these employees are more accessible and tuned in to the details of the need you are trying to address. Unfortunately, that command of detail may not necessarily do you any good.

The quadrant in the lower left corner of Figure 3.2 is reserved for the Non-Influential Non-Authoritarians (NINAs). These are some of the people you will find at the lower levels on the organization chart. They have no authority over matters such as determining how to spend the budget, selecting a supplier, or hiring team members. They have not yet established enough credibility to persuade those in power to seek out their views and give them an informal role in important matters.

This does not mean that they are not intelligent or unworthy; many times, they are extremely bright, dedicated, and talented professionals. Through personal choice or a function of their experience, they are followers at the point in time when your sales cycle is occurring. An organization relies on them to carry out certain functions but restrains them from taking any significant initiative—at least for the time being.

To get anything accomplished in an account, either before or after a sale, you have to work with NINAs quite a bit—if not for the majority of the time. Although they are important, *they do not drive sales.* They service their company's needs. And when you as a seller work with them, you are only servicing demand, which is vastly different from creating demand and providing a customer with Unexpected Value. Demand creation is the highest form of advanced selling and is the subject of Chapter 10. It enables you to work where you want to work and to set the pace for the competition. However, you cannot do it if you work only with NINAs.

This is a common trap into which many sellers fall: they end up spending the majority of their time with NINAs. They rely on them alone for direction and guidance, neither of which the NINAs can reliably and consistently provide. After all, they have a restricted role, and at times, do not know their own limitations. Most sellers at one time or another have had a NINA say something to them like, "I'm responsible for the evaluation, and I will be making the decision. You won't need to deal with anyone else. And frankly, I would prefer that you do not approach my management, since they have assigned *me* this task."

Is this person trying to boost his ego at your expense? Maybe; or perhaps his manager *wants* him to feel completely responsible for the project because the company can get a strong commitment in return from him if he does. Nevertheless, a manager's confidence goes only so far. In the 11th hour, as an evaluation peaks, management may well influence the decision, steering it in the direction *they* think is best. This may involve factors that were never introduced to the NINA—not through any fault of his, but simply due to the ways things played out.

So when you hear those words from a NINA, we suggest you check yourself for wounds—because you are bleeding. It's highly likely that somewhere in the organization, some competitor is dealing with an influential person who knows what the *real* buying criteria are; this person can shape the criteria to favor a particular supplier if he or she sees that it is in the company's best interest to do so. The revised specifications will eventually be passed down to your contact, but you won't learn about them until it is too late and the order has been placed with your competitor. At that point, it's easy to be left feeling that it was not fair because no one ever mentioned the new specifications; however, when you ask your NINA contact about it, he looks just as surprised as you.

Influence without Authority

The good news is that not all people who lack authority also lack influence. In the lower right-hand corner of Figure 3.2 are the Influential Non-Authoritarians. These people have established themselves as credible resources to those in authority for assisting in setting direction, establishing policy, forming standards and expectations, or simply acting as a sounding board.

Those who are driving organizations must create a support system for themselves. It is a matter of survival for them to delegate; by doing so, they extend their capacity. They become able to indirectly accomplish things that time constraints prevent them from achieving directly. Some delegated matters that are ordinary and routine can be handled by just about anyone. However, other matters are so critical that they must be assigned to those employees who are trustworthy and possess the expertise to get the job done. Non-Authoritarians become influential when they demonstrate that they can be trusted to carry out such important duties and produce the kind of results desired by those in higher positions.

Moreover, the influence of these individuals grows when they perform in a *manner* that management values. As a result, their supervisors assign them to other high-value responsibilities and seek their input on key issues. This is why people compete for "plum" projects—not because they are easy, but because succeeding at them builds for the future. And it is this success that enables people to become part of the Power Base.

Practically speaking, Influential Non-Authoritarians in today's world of selling can be any of the following:

- Heads of staff
- Trusted executive assistants
- Seemingly more junior employees that worked with an Influential Authoritarian at another company
- People who have significant expertise that is acknowledged by a powerful manager

This last one is the case with sellers who have achieved Customer Advisor status. This is where *you* should aim to be.

INFLUENCE IS CONSTANTLY CHANGING

The Power Matrix is a fluid, living chart in your customer organizations that is changing constantly. That is why it is important to understand *how* to identify influence, a topic we'll address later in the book.

For example, the first edition of *Power Base Selling* used the example of the United States government to explain the Power Matrix in Figure 3.2. We described the President as an Influential Authoritarian, the Vice President as a Non-Influential Authoritarian, and the First Lady as an Influential Non-Authoritarian. However, even in the time since the first edition was published, there have been several instances when all of these claims could be debated. We have seen times when Vice Presidents appeared to exert significant influence and other times when Presidents had to conduct a press conference to say that they were still relevant in the legislative process. This brings in the situational element that we will discuss shortly.

Another example is the discussion of who has wielded the most power in Russia. The Constitution of the Russian Federation makes it clear that the President is the head of state and has maximum authority and influence, yet few would dispute that Prime Minister Vladimir Putin really called the shots. Although he had less formal authority in comparison to President Dmitry Medvedev, he had disproportionately more influence.

What's the point of all this? Simply that:

Determining who has influence is not easy.

Knowing who is influential in sales is akin to knowing who needs to be sold on how your solution will improve your customer's business better than competitive alternatives. Great sellers understand that a sales campaign will involve many customer individuals. However, sellers can distinguish themselves by understanding the need to disproportionately focus on the few who have the influence to make things happen.

Let's look at a practical example that outlines how these concepts become important in everyday selling.

Meet Pat. He sells consulting services. His partner, Jake, briefed him for a customer meeting: "This deal is in the bag. The HR VP Joanne told me it was her decision and she wants to start. Let's try to secure a follow-up with the VP of Sales, Frank, who has a lot of influence." Pat asked Jake who else would be present. "A new business unit person named Courtney may call in and a junior guy named Daniel may be there. Joanne told me not to worry about them."

Because the customer second quarter (Q2) earnings call highlighted its business model transformation from products to services, Pat asked Joanne about this while walking into the meeting. She had no opinion. He then asked the VP of Sales about it while setting up for the meeting, and the VP indicated that he didn't think it would work. The meeting starts. Courtney, who is in the room as it turns out, speaks up right away and asks a question of Daniel. Although Joanne tries to jump in, Courtney interjects, "Joanne, would it make more sense to have this meeting after we assess our needs for the new business model? How about we circle back in six months?"

As the meeting winds down, everybody leaves except Pat and Daniel. "How long before Courtney is the new business unit head?" asks Pat.

"A few months," Daniel replies.

"How long before she replaces Frank?"

"Probably about 10 minutes after that," Daniel admits.

Pat then asks, "You previously worked for Courtney at Accenture and have been her eyes and ears during this transition, correct?"

"It was McKinsey," Daniel smiles.

To which Pat says, "Can we start over? I would like to discuss how we could help you and Courtney assess the requirements necessary to evolve from product to services."

"Great, because we need help," Daniel says, pulling up his calendar to set up a date for a meeting.

Pat showed great selling ability in this example. He was able to identify exactly who had influence—Courtney and Daniel—and who did
not—Joanne and Frank. However, like a majority of sellers, Jake wanted
to believe Joanne had influence because she was accessible and supportive.
Although this is a natural assumption, it's not always an accurate or fruitful
one, as we saw in this case.

What would have happened if Pat did not dive into customer politics
and identify influence? Our experience tells us that if in Pat's shoes, some
sellers would have stopped the sales cycle, walked away, and likely missed an
opportunity to create demand with Courtney and Daniel.

However, a majority of sellers would likely pursue a more costly
route. They would fail to pick up on the Power Struggle between Courtney
and Joanne, or the fact that Frank was outside the Power Base. Therefore,
they would pursue a follow-up meeting with Frank and Joanne. And as we
all know, it sometimes takes a few weeks to set up meetings; preparation and
travel are often involved. In addition, Joanne and Frank are apt to ask for
follow-up at the meeting that takes more time and effort—and will likely
have no consequence.

Essentially, not only would this path cause a seller to lose the deal, but
it would mean that he spent a lot of time and money losing the deal—all
because he did not want to get involved in customer politics.

DEGREES OF INFLUENCE

To make these concepts usable in everyday selling, we define three categories or levels of influence. We will refer to these definitions throughout the
book, and they are summarized in Figure 3.3.

1. **Foxes** are the center of influence within the Power Base.
2. **The Power Base** is a network of individuals within an organization who all have one thing in common: *influence*. It may come
   from authority or via association with authority; either way, they
   are powerful people who communicate and collaborate within the
   network.
3. **Those outside of the Power Base** are individuals without influence as it relates to your sales opportunity. They may be skilled, well
   intentioned, and hardworking, but they do not have the power to
   shape the purchasing decision.

Figure 3.3
Degrees of Influence

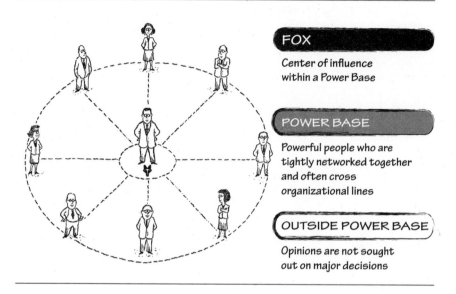

FOX

Center of influence
within a Power Base

POWER BASE

Powerful people who are
tightly networked together
and often cross
organizational lines

OUTSIDE POWER BASE

Opinions are not sought
out on major decisions

This chapter started our journey toward mastering politics by presenting the difference between influence and authority—and seeing the various places where both might exist within an organization. Next, we'll focus on customer Foxes—the center of influence and the heart of the Power Base. These high-integrity individuals place their organization first, often by *shaping* customer politics. Rarely surprised by events, Foxes work behind the scenes to prewire or shape decisions, often long before they are made. Foxes are high performers who are interested in getting the best out of the people around them, and our deal review experience shows that creating Political Advantage starts with them.

CHAPTER 4

FOXES

THE HEART OF THE POWER BASE

With foxes we must play the fox.

—Dr. Thomas Fuller

After the hero has saved the day and put all the villains securely behind bars, grateful citizens turn to thank him, but he is gone in an instant, no longer there to be thanked. The job is finished, and there is no time for public glory if you are . . . Batman. Yes, Batman. The archetype of the understated hero has always existed in literature, film, and storytelling. Characters like Robin Hood, the Lone Ranger, and Batman are just a few that we've seen win battles for the public good. They are fun to watch because they win with a sense of elegance and style.

Certain people in organizations are a bit like that, in a way. It's not because they have a penchant for being mysterious. It's simply that they have practical reasons for working quietly, behind the scenes, while less skillful fighters engage in noisy, public confrontations. In the world of selling, we call these understated achievers Foxes.

We use the term Fox not only because the label is fun and easy to remember but because foxes in the wild demonstrate wise and highly effective behavior that separates them from other animals. Certain characteristics come to mind when you envision foxes in their natural habitat. They're known as intelligent, clever, and resourceful creatures that are able to out-think—outfox, if you will—their opponents. They are quiet and patient and know the value of keeping a low profile.

Foxes combine astute observation with indirect methods to defeat competitors with a sense of style. For example, most wild animals that find themselves with fleas do the obvious thing and start biting and scratching.

It is a direct approach that not only is ineffective but can damage the skin and lead to infections and even more discomfort. Taking this approach within an organization would be akin to an individual attempting to advance his or her own interests in a way that damages the company as a whole. The best solutions—in the wild and in business—are always the holistic ones that protect the environment within which a problem resides.

Foxes know this and are also aware of fleas' vulnerability: they cannot swim well and drown when submerged in water. So when foxes have a problem with fleas, they simply find a stick and go for a swim. They carry the stick in their mouths, knowing that the fleas will start moving up their backs, onto their heads, down their noses, and onto the stick. The fox is patient and delights in watching the fleas move to the stick. Then, he simply releases the stick and watches the swarm of fleas drift off into confusion.

Human Foxes display many of the same traits in organizations. They become the center of influence and heart of the Power Base, not only because they are high performers who want the best for their organizations, but also because they understand how to appropriately leverage influence and authority to win with style—an approach that compels their organization's political structure to revolve around them. Foxes are high-integrity individuals who place their organization first. They're rarely surprised by events and work behind the scenes to prewire or shape decisions, often long before they are made. They are astute observers who plan ahead and see around corners.

Figure 4.1
The Fox Is Powerful

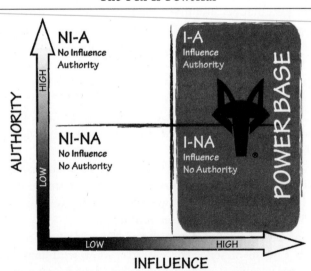

Note: The Fox image in Figure 4.1 is a registered trademark of Holden International.

Foxes are the most powerful customer individuals for sellers to know. As Figure 4.1 shows, Foxes occupy a space in the right-hand quadrant. We show it in the middle of the quadrant, but it can be anywhere from the upper portion of the quadrant to the lower portion of the Power Matrix introduced in Chapter 3.

Understanding how to work with Foxes is a critical part of creating Political Advantage. It is the fuel that enables sellers to provide unexpected customer value and defeat the competition. However, there's a somewhat ironic fact about Foxes' existence: the more powerful and truly foxlike they are, the harder they are to detect. But the trained eye can see that they leave behind their own version of fox prints (see Figure 4.2).

Figure 4.2
Getting Your Value to the Fox

A FOX IN ACTION

Let's use a practical example to illustrate how to detect and work with a Fox. Caroline Miller is the Vice President of Marketing at a medium-sized manufacturing company. Her role in the company has grown to such an extent that she is the most influential member of the Power Base—the Fox, as seen in Figure 4.3. Also notice that there's something a bit odd about this Power Base: while Manufacturing Department member Claire Thomas is part of the Power Base, Manufacturing's Vice President, Steve Kramer, is not. This indicates that in some respects, Claire

Figure 4.3
The Fox at the Heart of the Power Base

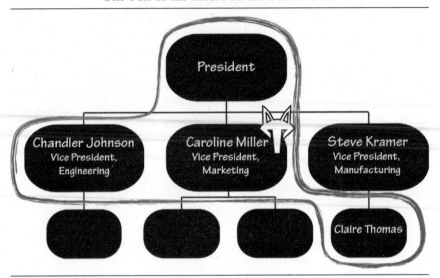

is more influential than her boss in the overall scheme of corporate affairs—which poses an interesting situation. How might this have come to pass?

Five years ago, Caroline traveled to Boston to attend a class reunion at her alma mater. One of her favorite professors introduced her to a graduate student named Claire Thomas. It did not take more than an hour-long lunch for Caroline to see that Claire was bright, was articulate, and had the confident air of a young woman decidedly on her way up in the world. Caroline offered her a summer internship at her company and Claire accepted.

Upon graduation, Claire joined the company's Marketing division full time. For the next year and a half, Claire established herself as a valuable resource in her division. She won the respect of many of the company's senior managers and earned a reputation in the field as being one of the rare people in the headquarters' office who could get things done. When a management position in Marketing became vacant, Caroline Miller's decision about who to promote was simple—and Claire adapted to the management role with ease. By watching Caroline in action, she had learned a lot about how to keep an organization running smoothly, even in difficult times. Now she also had a chance to try some of her own ideas.

Over the next two years, Claire developed her department into one of the most highly visible units in the company. Then, she changed jobs within the company. She took the position she now holds, managing a group in *Manufacturing*. So what happened here? Why, after "discovering" Claire and developing her for five years, did Caroline Miller simply hand her over to Manufacturing?

You can imagine what many people in the company thought: Claire Thomas's star had fallen. But take another look at the illustration of the Power Base in Figure 4.3. Claire is a Power Base member. She is influential. Her move would not only cross-train her on Manufacturing but would also bring new thinking to the Manufacturing group that she was to lead. It was an enhancement to the company, an exciting challenge for Claire, and a positive reflection on Caroline.

Claire's presence in Manufacturing provided Caroline with a trusted ally who was a crucial part of building a stronger relationship between the divisions—something that was necessary in order for the company to become more customer-centric.

Speaking of that, we should tell you something else about this organization: the Vice President of Manufacturing is going to retire in about 18 months. Who do you suppose is his heir apparent? You guessed it— Claire Thomas, whose elevation to an executive position will be as advantageous to the company, herself, and Caroline Miller, as was her move to Manufacturing in the first place. As we examine Caroline's motivations, we see two principles at work:

1. Always protect and strengthen the company.
2. If you manage the environment, you influence everything within it.

Figure 4.4 highlights the key attributes of a Fox.

Figure 4.4
The Fox

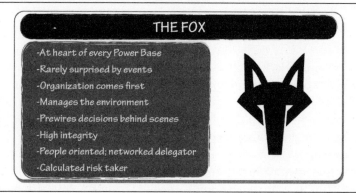

THE FOX

- At heart of every Power Base
- Rarely surprised by events
- Organization comes first
- Manages the environment
- Prewires decisions behind scenes
- High integrity
- People oriented; networked delegator
- Calculated risk taker

THE ORGANIZATION COMES FIRST

Caroline is motivated by the fact that the company is stronger and more customer-centric with Claire in an executive position. All true Foxes operate in such a manner, with their actions governed by the belief that everything they do must strengthen the organization in some way.

Foxes who do not live by this maxim are not really Foxes. They may have a lot of the same characteristics and seem every bit as intelligent, strategically oriented, and resourceful as Foxes. However, they are not Foxes if they do not put the organization first; instead, they are what we call *Jackals*.

The challenge is that on first glance, foxes and jackals have a lot in common. They look alike. Jackals are also monogamous and clever. However, it becomes apparent upon closer examination that key distinctions exist between the two both in terms of physical features and personal characteristics. The jackal's tail is longer, and its fur is not as smooth and shiny as the fox's. While a fox hunts living prey for food and plans ahead by storing rations in case of emergency, a jackal will eat anything, dead or alive—often feeding on another animal's catch and ignoring the inherent risks of disease. Jackals do not think ahead; rather, they maximize short-term gain, often with as little effort as possible.

When you translate this into the world of selling, it is obvious that corporate Foxes engage in healthy Power Struggles while Jackals attempt unhealthy Power Plays—political competition that is not in the company's best interest. A corporate Jackal will advance his agenda at the expense of his company and members of his own Power Base, and particularly at the expense of his supplier—*you*. For example, corporate Jackals make Power Plays for more projects, staff, and budget only to build up their fiefdom and satisfy their ego. If you align with a Jackal, you will be his first line of defense; he'll shift the blame to you if something goes wrong. The Jackal considers you to be an expendable supplier commodity. That's why you must always remember to:

Never mistake style for substance.

Unsurprisingly, Jackals tend *not* to endure. They are so nonholistic and destructive to their environment—the company—that others are ultimately able to see them exactly for what they are. It is then that senior management replaces them, leaving in their wake the damaged careers of good people. Certainly, there are times when you have to work with people who you don't trust, but it's wise to be careful and keep a safe distance when you do. If any customer individual tries to draw you into his or her organization's internal affairs in a case where doing so would be intrusive or inappropriate on your part, push back and gain some distance. Remember the example of the Jackal!

MANAGE THE ENVIRONMENT

Caroline Miller's second motivation in Claire Thomas's promotion is that she enhances her influence at the executive level of the company. At times, Foxes make success look effortless, simply because they maneuver so well behind the scenes. But another contributing factor to their apparently easy victories is often that they have shaped the environment to the extent that they know exactly which levers to pull in any situation.

Imagine that everyone in Caroline Miller's company agrees that they need to introduce a new product; however, they cannot reach a consensus about what the product's capabilities and specifications should be. In fact, there are two divergent points of view: one faction is headed by Chandler Johnson, the much-admired Vice President of Engineering who favors the introduction of a product that will be the most technologically advanced of its kind. It will seize the high end of the market and stake the company's claim to an entirely new sector through innovation.

In the other camp is Marketing. Caroline Miller is as aggressive as anyone else about the company's place in the industry, but she is not persuaded that the product Chandler Johnson's Engineering division has in mind is the wisest choice. She is all for innovation and technological excellence; however, she feels that the market may not support the price that they would need to charge. She is also very concerned about the impact of long manufacturing lead times on customers.

The President of the company will have to make the final decision at an executive meeting. Imagine that you are present there. Chandler Johnson gives a 20-minute presentation about the new technology and product that he is proposing. It's clear that he has done his homework, as he puts forth a well-thought-out approach. The numbers seem to add up, and his case for innovation and leadership in the marketplace is compelling.

The President now gives the floor to Caroline Miller. She begins by saying, "I'm impressed with Chandler's proposal. It is creative and leverages new technology. Now, I have an open mind and want to jump ahead of the competition, but wonder if we shouldn't move in stages."

Is Caroline surrendering? Of course not. Any assertive person will be tempted to engage in head-to-head battles with the opposition. For some, it is sometimes fun to go with fists flying into a confrontation and let the chips fall where they may. The problem with this is that you can win the battle and lose the war—something that is not holistic or foxlike.

The clever fighter, on the other hand, excels at winning with ease and with as few casualties as possible on both sides.

Caroline continues, "As we have discussed, I am concerned about pricing, given the elasticity of demand for the new product, but am also sensitive to customer lead times. Since Manufacturing will dictate what those lead times are, I'd like to hear what Claire Thomas thinks."

At this point, there are two things that Claire must *not* do. First, she cannot stand up and say, in effect, "I vote with Caroline; after all, she is my mentor." Her credibility would instantly evaporate if her colleagues perceived her as someone who merely parrots Caroline Miller's point of view.

The second thing that Claire must *not* do is engage Chandler Johnson in a predatory fashion. If Caroline is trying to win the battle without inflicting needless wounds, Claire must not start a bloodbath. Fortunately, Claire has been a good student under the tutelage of a Fox.

"Like Caroline, I am impressed with Chandler's proposal and the new technology. And I find it exciting that we are looking at an opportunity to lead the market. No matter how we proceed, I guarantee that Manufacturing can handle it."

She walks to a flipchart with figures she had prepared, saying, "For the new product, I think we can keep the added capacity and retooling costs down enough to only need an increase in the operating budget of about 25 percent. I know that sounds high, but until our volume increases, we will not have scale of economy from a production point of view. The only other concern is the impact on delivery for the first year. The good news is that demand has been high on our existing lines, which has caused shipping delays that now exceed five weeks. The new product could exceed that in the short term, causing further customer satisfaction problems."

After some discussion, Caroline introduces a migration path approach that would reduce the amount of innovation in the new product at launch. Then, over time, they could add new enhancements to manage cost and manufacturing lead times, while providing customers with new value.

Now, imagine that you are the CEO. You can go with Engineering's proposal, spend 25 percent more, and add to the delivery problem. Or, you can go with Caroline's more conservative approach that ultimately gets to the same point with less cost and risk. Which approach would you endorse?

While this example might sound a bit simple, it emphasizes the point that Foxes drive collaboration within organizations through direct and indirect influence. Look at what happened here; no one attacked the Vice President of Engineering. Instead, the Fox applied principles of risk and cost management to alter the path to success, even though some of those risks existed outside of her organization. This example shows how:

A Fox can be a "walking environmental control system."

You can bet that Caroline Miller was certain Claire would hold up her end for all the right reasons and that the President would make a decision that was in the best interest of the business. Keep in mind that Caroline is a Fox by association with the President, with whom she has a good relationship. It is a given that she would have spoken with him informally long before they ever convened the meeting.

SURVIVAL

A Fox's inclination to quietly work behind the scenes is more than a matter of being able to keep one's ego in check. By any measure, it is an operating necessity; however, that doesn't mean it's easy. For some people, power is like a drug. They must use it to fulfill themselves—and the more they use it, the more they need it.

Let's look at Claire Thomas in our previous example. As her influence began to grow, she chose to exert it discreetly. If she flaunted her power by association with Caroline Miller, the positive perception people had of her might suddenly change. Many colleagues would likely cease to perceive her as confident; instead, they'd see her as *arrogant*. Instead of being astute, she could be considered *cunning*. She would not be someone who works well with others, but rather one who *uses* them. In short, there is a serious price to pay for being heavy-handed with influence.

The same challenges exist for Caroline Miller. While she already holds a senior position in her company and her influence cannot exceed her authority within her formal domain of marketing, she is still able to expand her reach beyond marketing. As long as she is addressing a marketing matter, she can be as visible and direct as she would like, but beyond that domain, she must remain largely invisible. The issue is not having influence; it's a question of how she uses it. Some managers like to be hands on or perhaps micromanage an organization, while others use their influence to guide and coach others—even letting them fail on occasion. This latter type of manager intends for his or her staff to drive success, while the power-hungry manager is concerned only with success that resides with himself or herself—an approach that ultimately limits productivity and morale.

Caroline demonstrates discretion and respect outside of marketing so that others do not view her as being out of bounds. No matter how well-intentioned she may be, the organization will not tolerate an invasion into someone else's backyard unless she is subtle. There is a not-too-fine line between influencing the affairs of others and meddling. One needs to stay on the correct side of it by acting in an appropriate manner.

FOX FOOTPRINTS

All Foxes possess several common qualities. For starters, they are greatly respected for their wisdom, judgment, and ability to get things done. They are the kind of people whom others approach for their thoughts on significant matters, even if they are not directly involved in them. People call on Foxes for guidance and direction and regard them so highly that Foxes become amazingly well-connected. In fact, if there ever was a precursor to social networking in the corporate environment, it was within the domain or Power Base of Foxes—who are always in the know. Just as it is hard to sneak up on a fox in the wild, it is equally as unusual to catch a corporate Fox off guard in terms of any important matters within an organization.

Let's examine a few specific qualities that typify Foxes. Being able to identify these will help you determine foxlike behavior more accurately and quickly. It will also give you clues as to who is in the Fox's Power Base. But remember that this process is a lot like being invited to join someone's network in social media; merely finding Foxes is not the end goal. You can get close, but you cannot get in without an invitation. As such, building a relationship with a Fox is a privilege.

INTEGRITY

Foxes do not consider there to be gray areas when it comes to ethics. Everything here is black and white; one either has scruples or one does not. While, for example, a slightly padded expense report may not seem like a big deal to some people, it is to a Fox. As far as the Fox is concerned, it is indicative of the extent to which a person is guided by certain principles.

Foxes are also very much oriented toward the long term; as a result, they place a great deal of emphasis on things that endure. They look for quality in everything, including people. And quality people are those who have integrity, just as Foxes do.

PEOPLE-ORIENTED

Being people-oriented is as important as being company-oriented for a Fox. Because Foxes are value-driven, they know that value comes from people. Therefore, they excel at building relationships. Certainly, there is value in results—in work that is accomplished when projects are completed successfully. But a Fox knows that *people* get the results and complete the projects.

That insight alone can explain some curious behavior you may observe at work from time to time. For example, a Fox might give high priority to some project that, by any objective measure, should receive very little emphasis. This would confuse a lot of people, but the Fox's thinking is clear. While the project in question may have little significance by *itself*, the project team will gain valuable experience by tackling it. The Fox may see that somewhere down the road—perhaps even in a year or two—the organization will need that expertise.

Again, Foxes know that value comes from people and that people grow best when they are challenged. That is why you will consistently find that Foxes are good delegators. They know that entrusting responsibilities to others will expand their capacity to get results. However, they also know that when they delegate something, they also relinquish a certain amount of control. That is why many managers have difficulty doing this; and often the more important a task, the harder it is for most managers to assign it to someone else. They worry about whether they trust someone else enough to leave this matter in their hands.

How do you suppose a Fox makes such a determination? Your thoughts probably are heading in this direction:

A Fox will delegate to people who have proven themselves or have the potential to perform and will assign something important to *someone in the Power Base*.

So, every time you find out to whom a matter of substance has been delegated, you get a clearer picture of the Power Base of an organization.

RISK ASSUMPTION

In the same way that clever fighters make things look easy, Foxes are often risk takers who actually appear to be rather conservative. You have probably heard the term "calculated risk"; this means the following to a Fox:

Risk = Responsibility − Authority

In short, you are at risk in an organization when you accept responsibility to meet some objective but do not have the authority to marshal all the resources required to pull it off. And as we have already discovered, influence becomes critical when authority is lacking.

Think about how this applies to the way that Foxes interact with sellers. How responsible does your company hold you, the seller, for whether your customer buys your product? Unless you are in a very odd selling environment, the answer is "entirely responsible." Now, how much authority do you have within your customer account to make them buy? There should be no exceptions to this one: none. Therefore, your risk is 100 percent. You have all the responsibility and no authority. Let's look at it from your customer Fox's perspective.

Suppose you have sold your product to the Fox. How responsible does the Fox hold you for whether it does everything it is supposed to? Completely, right? How much authority do you have within your company to command all the resources it will take to make the product succeed—now and in the future? Sellers do not often have the formal authority to direct the efforts of Manufacturing personnel, Shipping supervisors, and Support resources. Once again, you have all the responsibility and none of the authority. As before, your risk is 100 percent.

The good news is that a Fox knows this about you. He is aware that no matter how good a seller you are or how persuasive and knowledgeable about products you may be, he assumes a certain amount of risk in selecting a supplier. That is a given. Some people are willing to blindly accept risk; these are the same people who wonder why they keep getting burned by bad decisions. Foxes work to minimize risk to the greatest degree possible. And they do this by managing it.

So if a Fox knows that authority is out of the question, what do you suppose he or she will want to see that you have? You got it: influence. Despite your lack of authority, when you can demonstrate to a Fox that you have influence—that you are sufficiently connected within your organization to make things happen—you represent real value, because your level of influence diminishes the Fox's risk, as Figure 4.5 depicts.

Figure 4.5
The Seller's Value Lowers the Fox's Risk

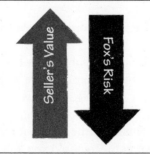

Let's say that Caroline Miller asks you to arrange a meeting with your company's CEO or secure certain resources to support a project. You know that it will most certainly test your level of influence within your company. As such, there is often a connection between the project's success and the amount of influence that the seller has—a situation that will dial the risk level up or down.

THE EMERGING FOX

Before we conclude our description of Foxes and transition to how to identify them, there is one last concept that is critical to understand—the *Emerging Fox*. This is a member of the Power Base who is on a trajectory to become a Fox in her or his own right.

Emerging Foxes just need more experience and time to build relationships and develop their foxcraft.

Figure 4.6
The Emerging Fox

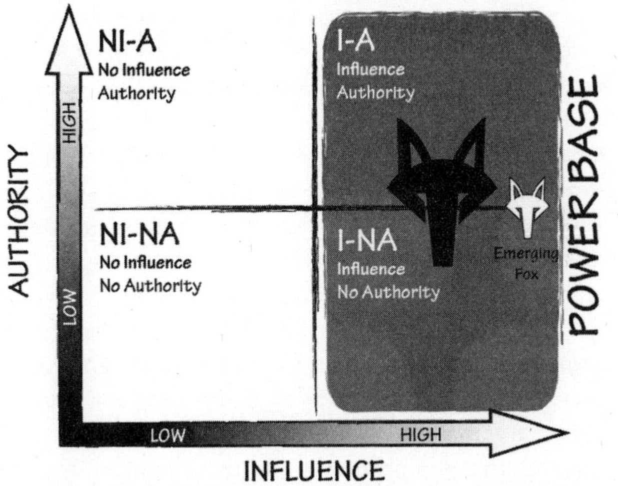

As Figure 4.6 illustrates, Emerging Foxes display all the qualities of a Fox but in subdued fashion. They have the integrity of a Fox but often have not had the opportunity to demonstrate it. While their people-oriented skills are visible to all, they generally don't have the relationships outside of their immediate Power Base to do a good job of mitigating risk through influence. They can change this by watching and learning from the Fox over time; and when they're ready, the Fox will actively help to forge these new relationships. All this occurs leading up to a point when the Emerging Fox will either move to a new part of the company or succeed the existing Fox.

Emerging Foxes are significant to sellers because they are frequently more accessible than the Fox. It's not that they have less to do or have more time on their hands; it is merely that they are typically very tuned into networking, as they actively build their careers. This openness and receptivity to credible people who may provide thought leadership is a hallmark of Emerging Foxes.

Sometimes, however, not all goes according to plan from the Fox's perspective. On the rare occasion, an Emerging Fox will attempt a coup, which takes the form of a Power Struggle or Play. At this point, politics really gets interesting from a seller's perspective. It's especially significant when your competitor is aligned with the Fox and you are counting on the Emerging Fox—in particular, his or her success in winning a Power Struggle—to assist you in penetrating the account. Again, this doesn't occur all that often; but when it does, an incumbent or installed supplier can become history in a short amount of time.

Now, there will not always be an Emerging Fox within a Power Base; however, there's usually one present somewhere. He or she may not be in the same department as the Fox, so don't limit your field of view by searching there; keep looking. You will want to reap the benefit of aligning with an Emerging Fox, while eliminating the risk of allowing a competitor to get to that person before you.

Let's look at a practical example where an Emerging Fox is central to advancing a sales campaign.

Meet Carlos. He sells business intelligence software and is trying to penetrate a large consumer goods company that has historically bought from his competitor. In fact, the CIO and customer Fox, Elizabeth, has twice signed a three-year contract with Carlos' competitor and is likely to do the same again in a few months.

Carlos believes that his product's ability to easily integrate with the customer's CRM system will provide more value to the customer than his competitor's product. However, Elizabeth will not make time for Carlos, partly because she is pleased with her current supplier and partly because she is extremely busy. Upon noticing this, Elizabeth's Power Base hasn't made time for Carlos either—and his time is, therefore, running out.

As a Stage IV Customer Advisor, Carlos identifies a customer IT Director named Eduardo who he believes is an Emerging Fox. Following a brief discussion, Eduardo agrees to a meeting. As it turns out, he is aware of the need to integrate with the CRM system in order to improve reporting, particularly to the finance group. However, he is not certain of Elizabeth's view on the subject.

Having said that, Eduardo is guided by the same principles or operating philosophy as Elizabeth. Specifically, he believes that one should always protect and strengthen the company and that managing the environment allows you to influence everything within it. This motivates Eduardo to take action. While keeping Elizabeth apprised of what he is doing, he gains the support of his company's finance team. Upon hearing of this new capability, the CFO approaches Elizabeth and asks her to consider CRM integration from a reporting point of view. He lets her know that it could be of significant value to his group.

Obviously proud of Eduardo's initiative and hard work, Elizabeth brings up the topic with him, and the two schedule a meeting with Carlos. As a result of that meeting, Elizabeth decides to open the bid, providing Carlos with an opportunity to compete—the first step in winning the business and taking the account from a competitor.

This is a great example because everybody wins if it works out (except, of course, Carlos' competitor). The customer benefits from increased reporting accuracy, Elizabeth enhances her relationship with the CFO, and Eduardo expands his network into finance, while also strengthening his relationship with Elizabeth—all as a result of Carlos' business savvy and political acumen.

The focus in this example was on the Fox and Emerging Fox, both of whom reside within a Power Base. The next chapter takes an in-depth look at these networks of influential people by characterizing them into their different types, while underscoring their practical significance in competitive selling. Think of the Power Base as the Bat Cave of customer politics.

CHAPTER 5

POWER BASE TYPES AND IMPLICATIONS

Sticks in a bundle are unbreakable.

—Kenyan Proverb

The previous chapter explained how Foxes appropriately leverage influence and authority to win with style. This simply means that they plan ahead and see around corners in order to achieve their goals without expending unnecessary effort or causing conflict. In fact, they even manage to build goodwill along the way.

Foxes are successful in part because they are able to work discreetly to predetermine critical decisions. What enables these powerful Foxes to work quietly behind the scenes while less skillful corporate players engage in noisy public confrontations? It is their ability to expand their personal capacity for achievement by delegating to people who have proven themselves. This process of delegation results in a network of high-performing individuals who revolve around the Fox. In other words:

Foxes *create* Power Bases.

This network of individuals becomes the organization's political structure— the Power Base—because they all have one thing in common: a significant amount of *influence*. A Power Base is a powerful force within any organization, capable of reaching across departmental and geographical lines where each Power Base member possesses the strength or influence of the entire Power Base. Some of this influence is derived from the authority that accompanies a person's position within a company. However, what can be even more important is the influence that Power Base members derive from others through relationships.

61

Chapter 4's example of Caroline Miller as the Fox exhibits how she attained a high level of influence by associating with her organization's President—someone who has significant influence from authority. Both individuals are members of the Power Base. In addition, others in the Power Base have increased influence from their association with the Fox, which raises the level of influence for all its members. When they speak, the Fox's voice is heard!

To summarize, influence within a Power Base is derived from:

- **Authority,** as is the case with the President and others in our Caroline Miller example.
- **Association with authority,** as is the case with Caroline, our Fox, and her relationship with the President.
- **Association with the Fox,** as is the case with Claire Thomas and Chandler Johnson (the Vice President of Engineering).

The architect, manager, and source of political strength of the Power Base is the Fox who is at the center of communications and collaboration within the network. As with the Fox, knowing how to work with the Power Base is essential to creating Political Advantage.

THREE TYPES OF POWER BASES

The first important point to understand about Power Bases is that organizations have multiple Power Bases—because organizations have multiple Foxes. Figure 5.1 outlines three distinct types of Power Bases that sellers must become proficient in navigating. Notice that the diagram also shows three Foxes, since each distinct Power Base revolves around a distinct Fox. Individuals in the diagram are characterized in terms of their authority and influence.

Figure 5.1
Three Types of Power Bases

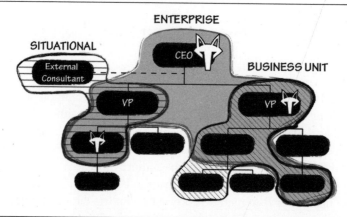

The Enterprise Power Base

The first type is the *Enterprise Power Base,* the group that sets the entire organization's direction and priorities, while also shaping its culture. It typically sits at the top of an organization chart with its members representing a subset of the corporate leadership team, starting with the Chief Executive Officer (CEO). As seen in Figure 5.1, it may also include influential people from certain business units or departments who can be at lower levels on the organization chart. It might also include individuals on the board of directors to whom the CEO reports.

We address how to identify who is in a Power Base in the next chapter, but a key point to make here is that it is absolutely crucial *not* to make general assumptions about who is in or out of a Power Base. For example, it is uncommon, but possible, for an organization's CEO to be absent from the Enterprise Power Base. One reason why this individual is a Non-Influential Authoritarian could be that he or she is getting close to stepping down or retiring, yet only a few key people are aware of it. Another reason might be situational in nature, in that the CEO simply chooses not to become involved in certain matters that are not part of his or her strategic or priority interests. Alternatively, the CEO may be delegating responsibilities, which is a foxlike characteristic, underscoring the need to avoid quick and general assumptions.

The Business Unit Power Base

The second type is the *Business Unit Power Base* (seen on the right in Figure 5.1). Essentially, each distinct unit or team of people will have its own Fox and, therefore, its own Power Base. This is true whether it is a line of business or a department, such as Engineering, Marketing, or Human Resources. As with the CEO, it is uncommon but possible for the formal leader of the business unit or team to be a Non-Influential Authoritarian.

The Situational Power Base

The third type is the *Situational Power Base* (on the left side of Figure 5.1). This is the most common—and challenging—Power Base for sellers to identify and navigate. Unlike its enterprise or business unit cousins, the Situational Power Base is far more dynamic and fluid in nature. Whereas the organization-centric versions are more stable over time, people move in and out of the Situational Power Base frequently.

So how do these informal and situationally driven networks of people form? Like their cousins, they are pulled together by a Fox; unlike the others, they operate under the cover of darkness. Situational Power Bases often extend horizontally across many organizational lines, crossing from one department to another. For example, a Senior Engineer in one department might, under the direction of the Fox, influence a Senior Engineer in another department, perhaps even in a different country; that engineer, in turn, influences a department head, to whom he or she reports, on a specific issue that is important to the Fox. Power Base members must take a great deal of care when exerting influence in this way so as not to usurp the authority of department managers. They accomplish this by exhibiting diplomacy, discretion, and respect for others.

A Situational Power Base is in some ways similar to a committee where individuals have been formally selected to come together as part of a cross-functional team or task force for the purpose of solving a problem or advancing some specific mission. At the same time, the members of these groups are also very different from one another. Comparing the Situational Power Base to a buying committee is a useful way to better understand this type of political network, given that buying committees are so common. As such, let's look at both the similarities and differences between a buying committee and an associated Situational Power Base—both of which have been formed because of an important upcoming acquisition:

- Both consist of a network of people with some likely overlap between the two.
- The Situational Power Base will often form before a buying committee is established and will therefore be able to influence who will participate on the committee.
- The Situational Power Base may consist of members who may not be on the committee but who will influence those on the committee.
- Like a buying committee, a Situational Power Base is cross-functional by definition and spans organizational lines.
- However, unlike a buying committee, the Situational Power Base carries a slightly different purpose. Instead of existing to solve a problem, for example, its general mission is to secure a specific solution to the problem. In other words, a buying committee's *real* decision-making power often resides with its companion Situational Power Base. People behind the scenes—along with certain influential individuals on the committee—are actually the ones who decide which supplier they'll choose. While the committee formally assesses all the business considerations, the Situational Power Base informally adds other political considerations that are important to the Fox of the Situational Power Base.

- The committee is formal in its nature and visible, whereas the Situational Power Base is informal and invisible.
- Wherever there is an important committee, there will often be a Situational Power Base, but there may not be a committee wherever there is a Situational Power Base.
- Those serving on a committee will generally remain in service for the life of the committee, whereas members of a Situational Power Base may come and go—something that can be positive *and* negative from a sales point of view.
- A buying committee may operate in a formally structured manner, particularly if involved with a public sector or government procurement effort, which greatly restricts what a seller can and cannot do during a sales campaign. However, a Situational Power Base does not operate according to any formal rules. Sellers, therefore, have the opportunity to create an influential Supporter to the extent that they can make contact with a member of the Situational Power Base who is not on the committee. Better still, if you can get to the Situational Fox before the committee is formed, your win probability will increase geometrically!

Of course, this is not to say that committees do not serve a purpose or provide value. They generally do good work and create buy-in or ownership of a recommendation, which is often crucial to successfully implementing the ultimate decision. But it's important to recognize that the true purpose committees serve, knowingly or unknowingly, is as political as it is functional.

Now, let's look at a sales example. An international company is considering consolidating the Information Technology (IT) Departments they have that currently reside in each country where they operate. Once they centralize IT, they will then outsource it. The company plans to evaluate several suppliers by conducting a rigorous and structured procurement process, but for now, they are focused on planning the IT transition. One supplier, whom we'll call Supplier A, is aware of the potential this situation presents and begins to play an active role in guiding the customer by working with its senior executives. They focus on the Enterprise Power Base, because no Situational Power Base has yet formed. They concentrate heavily on three areas:

1. The business and financial impact of the IT transition
2. The change management process to operationalize it
3. The business relationship between their company and that of the customer

Behind all this is a close alignment with the CEO, who is the Enterprise Fox. Company A knows that the CEO will be instrumental in forming the Situational Power Base, which, in turn, will determine who will be on the IT transition committee.

Fast-forward a bit into the future and the Situational Power Base is in place along with the committee, whose mission is to evaluate suppliers and select the best partner. Several new suppliers have entered the race at this point. One of them, Supplier B, is highly competitive given its size, reputation, and innovative business practices. For this reason, A is very concerned about B. Still, A is in the lead and has gathered political insight that B is just beginning to discover. Therefore, A's goal is to close the deal as quickly as possible.

The Situational Power Base consists of the CEO, who is the Fox, and each of four country managers, along with the Chief Information Officer (CIO) and Chief Financial Officer (CFO). The committee, on the other hand, is composed of a much larger population of people who span the ranks of executives, middle managers, and operations personnel.

As the sales situation begins to peak, the CEO meets with A and requests a very significant discount at the project's front end. Supplier A had developed a proposal that included a significant amount of consulting at the beginning in order to organize and implement the IT centralization. Now, the CEO wants a discount on that consulting work.

Supplier A works out an approach that's focused on being responsive and closing the business. They will provide the requested discount but will tie a performance fee to the back end of the deal. Supplier A's proposal states that it plans to outsource IT and thereby dramatically reduce the customer's IT expense. Knowing that their projected expense reduction numbers were conservative, Supplier A creates a performance payment for various levels of cost reduction over the outsourcing deal's 10-year period. They estimate that the amount of revenue generated by this approach will equal three times the discount being requested.

Everyone is happy. The CEO accepts A's approach, and A is confident that the business is theirs. "The competition has lost and they don't even know it," the A seller muses. In fact, it is hard for him *not* to think about the commission he's about to earn on this deal. Everything is proceeding so well; all he needs now is notification of the formal decision to proceed.

Then, something goes wrong. Supplier A's calls are not being returned, and the order is not forthcoming. As a seasoned seller, he knows that in the 11th hour of a sales situation, when you sense that you're in trouble, you often have a disaster!

A's instincts are correct. What he did not know is that two changes in the Situational Power Base have occurred. First, the CEO had exited the

Situational Power Base. As soon as A agreed to the discount, the CEO told his direct reports that they were to make the final decision and that they would be held accountable for its success. The last remaining significant risk had been taken out of the deal for him. Since he no longer needed or wanted to be in the Situational Power Base, he left it; and in doing so, he created a vacuum.

At that precise moment in time, the Emerging Fox within the Situational Power Base asserted herself. This individual was a country manager who did not want to lose control of IT in her country. As such, she immediately began to challenge A's approach, bogging them down with an endless cycle of dialog. Meanwhile, she consolidated support from the other country managers and soon became the Situational Fox. It was not long before the project was put on indefinite hold—the deal was dead!

How could something so good become so bad so quickly? Although the A seller had done a great job, he missed one area of vulnerability—not directly to a competitor, but to a no-deal decision by the customer. This might have been okay on its own, but because the A seller failed to identify the Emerging Fox and spend time with her to understand her views and priorities, the risk potential was high. In the absence of a relationship with her, it could have certainly created significant problems by itself if a competitor had gotten to the Emerging Fox. But that was not the case, since it was not a competitor that created the problem; it was the A seller himself.

When A's company agreed to provide the discount, they took the risk out of the deal for the CEO. It was that risk that kept the CEO in the Situational Power Base role as their key Supporter. In addition, a bit of over-confidence on the part of the A seller caused him not to see the opposition to IT consolidation within the customer's organization.

His mistake was twofold:

1. He viewed the Situational Power Base like one would an Enterprise or Business Unit Power Base: stable and changing slowly over time. However, we know that Situational Power Bases are far more dynamic.
2. He believed that giving the discount was a good thing to do, because he thought he was being responsive to the customer. However, given the Emerging Fox and her desire to kill the initiative, he was actually sealing his fate.

How do these different types of Power Bases relate to each other, and what does that mean from a seller's point of view? Successful account management requires that relationships be built with people in both the Enterprise and appropriate Business Unit Power Bases. *At least, this is the case if you define account management as the process of building competitive advantage away from products and services.* Sure, solutions are physically required to deliver significant value to customers; however, it is account management, as a Stage IV science, that leverages the value of those solutions to boost win rates and repeat business.

Customer Advisors competitively shape the environment within which orders are generated by preloading them with competitive advantage. At this level:

It all comes down to demonstrating thought leadership to advance the customer's business and having Power Base members recognize it. Then you are already aligned when an opportunity develops and a Situational Power Base springs to life.

This provides you with access to people, insight, and support that the competition can only dream about.

Let's look at another practical example.

Meet Jill. She is selling a $3 million software product to a large hospital that recently invested $50 million in a separate solution with a different supplier to automate patient records. After assessing the situation, Jill wisely determined that a Situational Power Base was quietly presiding over her sales cycle. She also knew who was most likely part of that Power Base, based on insight from having worked with customer individuals who were part of the Enterprise Power Base. Jill further understood that her product would have to support the broader patient records solution. As a result, she constructed an integrated solution.

Fast-forward several months. The Situational Fox is attending a meeting on an unrelated subject. The Enterprise Fox is also present, providing an opportunity for the Situational Fox to float an encapsulation of Jill's integrated solution with him. The response is positive.

Three weeks later, Jill is selected to be on the short list of potential suppliers. Two weeks after that, she is awarded the business. Competitors learn that Jill's company was chosen because of its comprehensive and cost-effective solution. Jill knows, however, that she was selected because of her account management skills, which combined political strength with business savvy to produce relative superiority.

In this example, we discussed the political mechanics at a high level. However, what motivated the Situational Fox to support Jill? Why was the Enterprise Fox responsive? Was it only because of the nature of the integrated solution, or was there more at play? These are key questions that we explore in Chapter 7. But for now, it is important to grasp how critical it was for Jill to identify multiple Power Bases and understand how they relate to one another and work together.

MAPPING THE POWER BASE

To deepen your understanding of working with Power Bases and the implications this has on how you should spend your time, let's dive into another example. Figure 5.2 shows an organization chart for the sales force of a medium-sized manufacturing company. This is the official structure, or distribution of authority. This chart tells you that the sales function is headed by a Vice President (VP) who has three Directors reporting to him: one each in the west, central, and east regions. Each of these Directors has a Sales Manager and a Support Manager reporting to him or her.

Figure 5.2
Sample Organization Chart (Distribution of Authority)

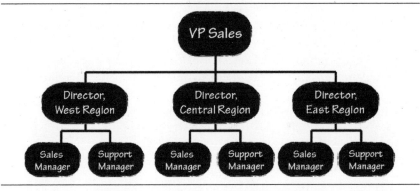

Along with background information on each of the players and some knowledge of perceived product needs, this chart would likely represent the sum total of Stage I and II sellers' insight into the account. Stage IV Customer Advisors, however, recognize that there is much more insight to be gathered. Behind this official structure is a political one, a Power Base of influential individuals who revolve around a powerful Fox.

Suppose you have gained political insight by applying what you will learn in Chapter 6 on how to identify Foxes and Power Base members. As a result, you determine that the sales VP is the Business Unit Fox. Next, you establish who may be in the Fox's Business Unit Power Base—and more important, how that insight will shape the way you spend your time in the account.

You know the VP is new to his position and has been drafted to the role by the CEO, with whom he worked previously at another company. You discover that he believes that he inherited a problem with the West Regional Director, and you learn that the VP helped the East Regional Director get his job even before he joined the company. You find out through discussions with others that he relies heavily on the Central Regional Director for advice on quotas and compensation incentives for new products.

You can now begin to draw a few hypotheses about the Power Base: for example, the Central and East Directors appear to have influence, whereas the West Director may not. You discover even more over time. The VP's lack of confidence in the West Regional Director has apparently caused him to rely heavily on the West Sales Manager, with whom he prefers to work directly whenever possible. You also find out that the Central Sales Manager is viewed as a good administrator but is somewhat unimaginative. On the other hand, the Support Manager there has demonstrated a flair for marketing. In fact, the VP has even asked him to comment on how to improve support programs throughout the entire company.

This additional insight has provided you with an even clearer vision of the Business Unit Power Base. The West Regional Sales Manager and the Central Regional Support Manager have obviously developed an association with the Fox that allows them to increase their own influence by association with the Fox, as Influential Non–Authoritarians. This places them in the Fox's Power Base. Figure 5.3 shows how.

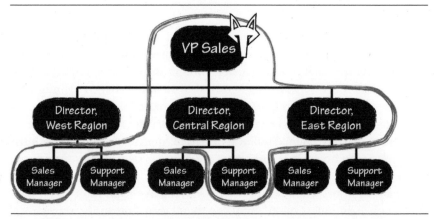

Figure 5.3
The Power Base (Distribution of Influence)

The Power Base can be overlaid on the formal organization chart. Doing this lets you make visible what is usually invisible and make tangible what is usually intangible. Whereas the organization chart depicts the distribution of authority, the Power Base depicts the distribution of influence.

POWER BASE IMPLICATIONS FOR SELLERS

Stage IV Customer Advisors focus on people with influence—the Fox and Power Base members—for two main reasons:

1. **To drive enhanced Value Creation and Competitive Differentiation.** As a result, they are better positioned to improve their customer's business and win more deals at a higher price. Again, this is due to the rich insight they develop from customer individuals who are "in the know"—or in the Power Base. This insight leads to enhanced value to customer and supplier alike.
2. **To succeed while spending as little of their own time and company money as possible.** Power Bases would not matter if you sold in a world without constraints. If you had the time and money to call on every customer individual before a decision was going to be made, you would. But you don't. Time and money are real constraints. And this approach addresses them accordingly.

Working with Foxes and Power Bases not only helps you win more deals but saves you time and money in terms of shorter sales cycles and reduced cost of sales.

To elaborate on this point, let's return to the example of the seller working on the account in the section titled Mapping the Power Base. The seller would make a huge error if he took direction from the West Regional Director, no matter how strong their relationship is. Even if the West Regional Director happened to be a formal decision maker on some matter, the real decision will be influenced by the East and Central Directors.

Imagine what could take place. Although well intentioned, the West Regional Director could provide inaccurate information; or worse, he could ask for future work that will not have a positive sales consequence. For example, the West Regional Director may inform the seller that he wants to see a demonstration of the product's ability to integrate with an existing product that they are using. In response, the seller spends time researching the integration request, coordinating with technical support personnel, and preparing to conduct the demonstration at the customer's facility. On top of that, the seller and support people may need to fly to the customer location, which will only add more time and expense.

Of course, all this could be very appropriate for the right deal. However, suppose that the Fox feels that integration with the existing product is not necessary. Perhaps there are other important considerations of which the West Regional Director is not aware since he's not in the Power Base. Sales time and costs go up, while win potential goes down. Selling to someone outside of the Power Base is like driving in a heavy fog without knowing it. Things *seem* to look okay. You're moving ahead and you know that the sales campaign is progressing, but in what direction? Like a pilot who has lost the horizon, this is a dangerous situation for a seller.

Avoiding the fog of selling and achieving Political Advantage requires that sellers quickly find people in the Power Base who are not always easy to find. The good news, however, is that when you discover a member of this political network that we call a Power Base, he or she can lead you to the Fox. Yet, this requires that you know *what* to look for, along with *when* and *how* to look for it. This is precisely why finding the Fox's Bat Cave is the subject of the next chapter.

CHAPTER 6

FOX HUNTING AND POWER BASE MAPPING

Nothing has such power to broaden the mind as the ability to investigate systematically.

—Marcus Aurelius

We find that although most sellers intellectually understand the significance of working with Foxes and Power Bases, they fail to develop the daily habits that allow them to quickly and naturally identify them. This gap between recognition and implementation tends to prevent sellers from gaining the coveted Political Advantage that fuels Value Creation and competitive strategy in their accounts. This chapter helps close this gap by showing you how to uncover certain Political Revelations to determine who is a Fox and who is inside or outside the Power Base. Over time, the activities that drive these Revelations will become a lot more natural and automatic for you to complete, and soon, they will become second nature.

We refer to this process as Fox Hunting because the focus should be on finding the Fox. Aiming for the Fox makes it easier to identify Power Base members along the way, which you often do even before you identify the Fox. That's okay; you will eventually need both, and members of the Power Base can help you recognize and align with the Fox.

We present Fox Hunting in two parts. We first provide a brief explanation of useful tools for the hunt, and then we show exactly how to apply these tools in order to make hypotheses and draw conclusions about a given individual's degree of influence.

FOX HUNTING INTELLIGENCE GATHERING

The best sellers rely on three primary Fox-Hunting activities to develop visibility into who may be the Fox and in the Power Base. These include:

1. Conducting customer research
2. Making astute observations
3. Asking good questions

These three tools are meant to be used *together* to help form hypotheses and draw conclusions about an individual's degree of influence. In other words, it's not enough to draw a conclusion based on *one* research item, observation, or question. All three tools are needed to connect the dots over time. Customer research provides sellers with information, while astute observations apply judgment or inference to that information. For example, let's say that a Chief Executive Officer (CEO) presents several company initiatives to industry analysts but spends more time and goes into more detail on one specific initiative. A seller therefore might infer that the initiative that gets most of the attention is his highest priority.

Asking good questions results in two outcomes:

1. Additional information in targeted areas, perhaps providing background on the CEO's initiatives, particularly the one that you feel is the highest priority
2. The ability to move from inference to conclusion, such as in confirming the high-priority initiative through questions addressed to other key customer individuals

We refer to this process, which is shown in Figure 6.1, as intelligence gathering or, simply, intel, and you will use it in this chapter for Fox Hunting, in Chapter 9 for developing customer value, and in Chapter 11 for gaining competitive intelligence.

Figure 6.1
Fox Hunting Intel Gathering

CUSTOMER RESEARCH   ASTUTE OBSERVATIONS   GOOD QUESTIONS

In each case it will advance you up the knowledge dimension of the Holden Four Stage Model presented in Chapter 2, which introduced the progression from Data to Information to Insight to Wisdom. You have heard the saying "information is power," and to an extent, this is true. But more powerful is insight, as it is far less common than information and carries more value. And so it is that influence is derived from authority or by association with authority, but it is also true that influence is produced by insightfulness and the wisdom to apply insight effectively.

Customer Research—What Information Can You Gather in 30 Minutes?

We are always surprised about how little sellers know about their customers' business nowadays, when there's so much publicly available information accessible on the Internet. "We don't have enough time to conduct research," sellers often tell us. Our response is that spending at least 30 minutes gathering key insight could save you hours of time talking about irrelevant topics to people not able to influence your sale—all of which cost you time and money.

The exact amount of time you spend researching depends on the size of the customer account. You may wish to spend more than 30 minutes for large accounts, whereas smaller transactional accounts might require less of your time. In either case, you will be amazed at how much insight you can gain quickly if you know where—and *how*—to look.

We specifically recommend the following six activities, which can be completed in about 30 minutes. Figure 6.2 provides a summary.

Figure 6.2
Six Customer Research Activities in 30 Minutes

	Source	Look For
1) List of Customer Executives	Website	Authority
2) Executive Biographies	Website	Themes/ Connections
3) Social Media Profiles	LinkedIn, Twitter and equivalents	Connections/ Recommendations
4) Public Presentations	Website	Who is presenting/ Key themes
5) News Releases	Website	Who is representing company/ New initiatives
6) Chairman's Letter	Website	Critical business issues

1. **Identify a preliminary list of customer executives within an account.** These are people who you feel are relevant to your sales efforts based on the customer's organization chart. You need to start with the distribution of authority before studying the distribution of influence, as the two are connected. This list should include the organization's top leaders, including the CEO, Chief Financial Officer (CFO), and the leader in charge of the functional area to whom you sell, for example, Information Technology (IT), Marketing, Engineering, and so forth. You can almost always find such a list on an organization's website, regardless of whether the company is publicly traded, privately held, or a public sector agency.

2. **Read executive biographies.** Read the biographies of just those listed on the organization's website. What do the organization and executive want you to know about each individual? By looking for themes, you can begin making hypotheses about the political network and culture. For example, is there a company where multiple executives worked together in the past? Was there a leader who departed and whom multiple executives followed? If so, you may have found a Fox print and associated network. Did many of the executives attend similar universities or study similar subjects? For example, if the top company leaders all studied electrical engineering, it is a safe bet that this could be a technology-driven company. Simple research like this prepares you to better map into the customer's organizational priorities, language, and culture.

3. **Study social media profiles.** The next thing you want to do is visit sites such as LinkedIn, Twitter, and Facebook and take the following actions:

   - Review the individual's profile, since this often includes information on work history and education. This is particularly helpful if there was not an official executive biography on the company's website.

   - Look at the person's contacts and connections. How many connections does the person have? Clearly, a long list of connections indicates that the individual is well networked. If the connections are publicly viewable, then take some time to scan through them. Who from the individual's current company is also a member of his or her social media network? Although this doesn't necessarily mean they are in a Power Base together, it is a data point to consider. Next, assess whether you have any shared connections—a person from both your networks in common. Any mutual connections would be helpful to talk with as you begin hypothesizing about the individual's degree of influence. Last, see if any themes emerge among the connections. For example, does the executive stay connected to one particular former company? If so, you can bet that he or she is well networked there.

- Take notice of virtual communities and/or "groups" to which the person belongs. This may point out what motivates and interests him or her.

4. **Look through the last two public presentations you can find.** Read any publicly traded companies' quarterly presentations to stock market analysts, since these can be rich with Fox-finding clues. Who is presenting? What key themes did they cover? What are they counting on to drive company growth? Companies that are not publicly traded often post industry conference presentations on their websites that include similar insight. Government agencies publish a wealth of information on their mission, structure, operations, budget, and more.

5. **Read the last five press releases.** Most organizations include a "news" section on their websites that can help you answer questions like the following: What does the organization want to broadcast about its strategy and people? What are the most recent initiatives? Who does the company trust to represent it in the public eye?

6. **Read the chairman's letter in the annual report.** The economic scrutiny of the past 10 years has transformed these short letters from fluffy marketing promotions into helpful documents that detail company strategy. This provides one succinct place for the organization to reveal its strategy for success and let people know who they are counting on to lead it. Equivalent documents usually exist on the websites of organizations that are private or part of the public sector.

Although we encourage you to invest more time because it will lead to better insight, you can complete these six activities in about 30 minutes. They will arm you with enough relevant information to prepare you to take advantage of the next Fox-Hunting tool: astute observations.

Astute Observations—Knowing What to Look For

You will want to make Fox Hunting a daily habit within your accounts, using your customer research as context for what you will see. Generally

speaking, people use influence—and therefore make it more visible—
during times of *change* within your customer's organization.

We like to say that:

Change illuminates power.

Many types of change shine a light on power structures; Figure 6.3
summarizes the most common examples of these. In addition to the
substance and implications of the communications listed, focus on "who"
is doing what.

Figure 6.3
Astute Observations During Times of Change

	Look For
1) Strategy announcements	Who is making the announcement?
2) Reorganization	Who is driving it?
3) Promotions and demotions	Who is rising or falling?
4) New hires	Who? From where? Others?
5) Mergers and acquisitions	Who is in charge?
6) Shifts in budget allocation	Who announced the shift? Who benefited?
7) New product introductions	Who is making the announcement?
8) Company awards	Who are the high performers?
9) External communications	Who speaks for the company?

1. *New strategy announcements or significant changes in company or departmental direction:* Who announced them? What drove the new
   direction?
2. *Reorganizations:* Who can articulate the business purpose driving the
   new structure? Who gained authority?
3. *Promotions and demotions:* Who is moving up? Who is moving out?
4. *Key new hires:* Who brought them in? From where? Are others
   coming?

5. *Mergers and acquisitions:* Who can explain the business logic of the merger or acquisition? Who appears to be in charge?
6. *Shifts in budget allocation:* Who announced the shift? Who benefited from it?
7. *New product introductions:* Who has been placed in charge?
8. *Company awards and special recognition:* Who are the high performers?
9. *External communications:* Who is trusted to represent the company publicly?

The combined insight from your research and observations will prepare you to maximize implementation of the most powerful Fox-Hunting tool—asking good questions.

Good Questions—How to Ask the Right Ones

"Judge a person by his questions rather than by his answers," wrote the Frenchman Pierre-Marc-Gaston in the 19th century. Gaston could very well have been talking about sellers because the ability to ask good questions is paramount for Stage III and IV selling. Great sellers are inquisitive listeners.

In a moment we cover *what to ask,* along with a list of actual Fox-Hunting questions. First, we want to cover *how to ask* the questions—because it has been our experience that questions used to identify influence have three key traits, which are summarized in Figure 6.4.

Figure 6.4
Gauging Influence

Characteristics of Questions to Gauge Influence

1) Lead with *your insight* or embed it into your question

2) Open-ended and following your insight statement, start with "What" or "How"

3) Best asked in informal settings

1. Good questions to gauge influence include relevant *insight* that you have derived from your research and observations. The question leads with your insight. This gives you credibility, which, in turn,

gives your customer confidence that taking the time to provide a thoughtful answer may enable you to provide additional insights. Therefore, a mutually beneficial dialog begins. For example, rather than asking, "What are your goals?" a Fox-Hunting question would be, "Given that your CEO announced that customer privacy is a top priority, *how* will that impact your goals to grow your online advertising business?" The latter question leads with your insight, which will result in richer dialog.

2. You should ask *open-ended* questions, rather than closed-ended ones, to gauge influence. Open-ended questions cannot be answered with a single word, such as "yes." They require more thought from the individual answering because they elicit explanation, opinions, and feelings. An example of a closed-ended question is "Has the budget been approved for this project?" An example of an open-ended, and therefore potentially more fruitful, question is, "What is your opinion on how the CEO will respond to the projected cost of this project?" A response might be, "I suspect that pricing, given the existing budget, will be less of an issue in comparison to how the purchase is made. Avoiding a capital expenditure with leasing or a pay-as-you-go service-based pricing structure would, in my view, be more attractive to our executives."

   Most open-ended questions begin with either "what" or "how." The most effective types of "what" questions inquire about goals, challenges, priorities, opinions, and feelings—for instance, "Given that your company is altering its business model to pursue a services strategy, *what* are your department's goals and challenges?" Another example is, "*What* is your opinion about your organization's decision to divest its hardware division?"

   Generally, the most effective types of "how" questions solicit the person's perspective on connecting a cause-and-effect relationship. An example is, "*How* will it impact your team if Mary brings Joe over from her previous company to lead the company's security initiative?" Another example is, "*How* does the recent decision to broaden your business model to include services impact your goal of 10 percent market share gain in China?" Whatever you say, or however you say it, remember to keep it open-ended and insightful.

3. It's best to ask questions designed to identify influence *informally.* When asking probing questions about personal opinions and feelings, sellers must recognize that people may not want to broadcast

their answers publicly. It is not a smart selling approach to ask these types of questions over a formal conference room table or among a group of people. They are best asked in less formal settings, such as walking from a customer's meeting room to the front lobby, during a round of golf, or over lunch.

If you are selling a relatively large ticket item, it is vital to interact *face-to-face* with your customer. Although the advances of email and video conferencing enable sellers to increase the frequency of customer interactions at a reduced expense, you should use them only to complement—not to replace—in-person account management. Critical subtleties in body language and expression, combined with increased opportunities for informal one-to-one conversations—for example, walking to a break room to get a coffee before the meeting starts—make in-person interaction an important vehicle for gauging influence.

These are the tools to use. Next, we show how to apply these tools in order to make hypotheses and draw conclusions about an individual's degree of influence.

POLITICAL REVELATIONS

Our experience in competitive deals suggests that Foxes use influence and reveal themselves during a number of specific situations. These are areas of Political Revelation upon which we rely for Fox-Hunting intel, as shown in Figure 6.5. Together, they help determine whether an individual is in fact a Fox, in the Fox's Power Base, or outside of the Situational Power Base for your particular sale.

We use the word *revelation* because the first few times a seller experiences this, it is exciting, profound, and relevant. Being able to recognize these situations creates "aha" moments that significantly advance your ability to add value to your customer and win deals.

We provide examples of Fox-Hunting observations or questions for each Political Revelation, highlighting just a few of many that best demonstrate practical implementation. There are times when you are able to see someone exerting influence in real time, for example, when an answer to a question or an observation in a meeting proves obvious. It is less common at other times to see individuals using their influence; in these situations, you need to play the role of detective and reconstruct what may have caused an outcome to occur. Just remember, there are no silver bullets, as identifying influence requires connecting the dots among multiple data points over time.

Figure 6.5
Fox–Hunting Intel

POLITICAL REVELATIONS: FOXES...

1) Help shape their organization's STRATEGY, PHILOSOPHY, AND CULTURE

2) Tend to work on projects that are STRATEGICALLY IMPORTANT to company's success

3) Are often shown subtle ACKNOWLEDGMENTS OF RESPECT by others

4) Are effective RISK TAKERS

5) Know how and when to appropriately and successfully WORK IN EXCEPTION TO COMPANY POLICY

6) Historically EXERT INFLUENCE OUTSIDE OF THEIR DEPARTMENT, division, or business unit

---

1. **Foxes help shape their organization's strategy, philosophy, and culture.** Foxes take ownership for the direction their team is taking and the values upon which it operates. These values translate to the Fox's Power Base members, who skillfully implement the Fox's vision. Individuals outside the Power Base are not always able to succinctly articulate the vision. However, this does not mean that working with individuals outside the Power Base is not important to your sales cycle. These individuals may be a good source of information about well-defined initiatives, such as stated buying specifications. Just keep in mind that they are likely not aware of major decisions or shifts in thinking or planning that the Fox may be considering.

FOX-HUNTING QUESTION

"How does the recent decision to pursue a new type of customer base support your stated goal of achieving 30 percent market share in Western Europe?"

A Fox, responding to this question, likely would describe why he made the decision to change the type of customer his company was targeting. He would have specific insight into the business impact anticipated from the change and the ability to link it to the market share goal. Power Base members would be in the know relative to the Fox's plans and priorities, particularly as they relate to implementation details. However, they may not be able to explain the full reasoning behind them. Individuals outside of the Power Base would probably not be interested in engaging on this topic in any depth with you, as they may be more focused on immediate action items.

In this simplified example, as with all subsequent examples, you will need to ask several follow-up questions; there is never one question that will reveal everything you need to know.

2. **Foxes tend to work on projects that are strategically important to their company's success.** In other words, Foxes go where the action is, drafting other members of the Power Base as appropriate. They do this for two reasons:
   a. To create maximum impact for the company. Their involvement is often sought after in many areas, but they tend to be selective in terms of where they'll concentrate their efforts.
   b. To go beyond what is expected and deliver more than what management has requested. By focusing on the most important projects, they provide Unexpected Value that produces growing recognition by the right people, which strengthens relationships for themselves and the Power Base members that they draft into such projects.

Individuals outside the Power Base, on the other hand, are not purposely trying to find such projects. In fact, they are often attempting to avoid this kind of extra work.

FOX-HUNTING QUESTION

"I noticed that the last three public speeches by your CEO have focused on the business model shift to cloud computing. How do you feel about this shift, and what will be your level of involvement in it, if any?"

When answering this question, a Fox would likely comment on why cloud computing is particularly important to the company and how its approach differentiates his company from the competition. If you have earned the Fox's trust, he may confide in you that he is on a special companywide task force to ensure the initiative's success. A Power Base member might relate a discussion he had with the Fox, in which the Fox asked him to support the initiative. Someone outside of the Power Base would likely say something like, "I didn't notice, but it makes sense, as that seems to be where the industry is going."

3. **Foxes are often shown subtle acknowledgments of respect by others.** You may notice that when a Fox speaks during a meeting, everybody pays careful attention. The Fox's influence becomes visible. At other times, people will seek advice from the Fox even though the topic is outside of the Fox's formal responsibility. Such interactions acknowledge the Fox's power and wisdom. Foxes also seek out opinions of Power Base members, whereas opinions of individuals outside of the Power Base are less sought after.

FOX-HUNTING OBSERVATION

Carefully observe body language and other visible signs during meetings. You might notice that others sit up straight and become more focused when one particular person enters the room. That same person may make a simple comment that changes the direction of the meeting or people's opinions.

This Revelation is an example of one that you can usually observe in real time, underscoring how helpful it is to have face-to-face interaction during important sales cycles. When considering this data point among other insight gained from your intel, you may hypothesize that this person could be a Fox. Suppose that the Fox seeks out one specific person in the room and asks his or her opinion on an important topic. What could that mean? Alternatively, what does it mean if an individual constantly brings up a particular subject, which the group repeatedly fails to engage?

4. **Foxes are effective risk takers.** Foxes will often sign up to lead companywide initiatives that have strategically important missions but uncertain outcomes. They are motivated to make a big impact. Power Base members will also take risk, but if it is significant, it will almost always be with the support of the Fox. Individuals outside of the Power Base will generally avoid risk but will sometimes assume

risk without being aware of it. For example, when such a person, even unknowingly, opposes the direction of a Fox, correction, reassignment, or worse can be the outcome.

Foxes are definitely not risk-averse, but that's not because they are some kind of heroic figure. It is that they see risk in a different way, which can make an uncertain outcome look a lot more attractive. They will take on risk if it meets two requirements:

a. The magnitude of the risk must be reasonable and consistent with the reward at hand.

b. The risk must be manageable.

High amounts of risk can be acceptable if accompanied by an ability to influence the risk. And that is where members of the Power Base, and great sellers, come into the equation. They help manage risk, often with their expertise. They become risk mitigators!

Fox-Hunting Question

"I am excited about the new security platform vision that you and the cross-company task force are leading. It makes a lot of sense to eliminate the need to secure each piece of software and each device on the platform, and it will also strengthen overall security and reduce the cost of development. At the same time, however, the entire platform will be compromised if a security breach does occur. How do you feel about this type of platform-level risk?"

A Fox would likely acknowledge the astute observation and discuss how the approach will be managed. He might also refer to past projects or other examples where he's achieved (or is achieving) success. Power Base members would be aware of the project and supportive of the Fox. On the other hand, individuals outside of the Power Base would likely not have thought through the risk issues and would rely instead on departmental management while focusing on the project's operational considerations.

5. **Foxes know how and when to appropriately and successfully work in exception to company policy.** Foxes have both the political strength and the wisdom to discern when an exception to policy is warranted. They also know how to go about acting upon it to advance long-term company success. Again, they rely on support from their Power Base and, over time, earn more

and more credibility from the right people in the company. Power Base members operate in exception to policy (on a limited basis) with support from the Fox, while individuals outside the Power Base are more likely to follow departmental policy and guidelines to the letter.

FOX-HUNTING QUESTION

"Mary, I see that you are hiring a new Director of Marketing for the business unit; however, I was under the impression that a hiring freeze was in place?"

The Fox Vice President (VP) might answer in the following way: "You are right; we do have a freeze in place, along with a number of other cost-reducing measures. But we also need to advance our plan to reach $8 billion within three years. As I think you know, our business unit is leading that effort, and this hire is a critical part of both the business unit and the company's strategic plan."

Although Foxes can and *do* work in exception to company policy, they don't do so in an arrogant or inappropriate manner. Rather, they do so with justification and credibility. In our example dialog, Mary links the new hire to the extended strategic significance of advancing the company's growth goal. Instead of seeing this as noncompliant to policy, the individuals involved view it as real leadership. More often than not, people witness Power Base members supporting a Fox; in this regard and on the rare occasion, you may see them acting in exception to policy in order to do so. However, individuals outside of the Power Base would not even conceive of acting against a company directive.

6. **Foxes have a history of exerting influence outside of their department, division, or business unit.** We saved this Revelation for last because it requires the most advanced understanding and application of politics. On one hand, of all the Revelations, it may most definitely identify a Fox. An individual's degree of influence reaches its height of intensity when it can determine outcomes within another person's area of authority. A Fox intervenes in another person's area of authority either because the person has requested it or because the Fox believes that his or her involvement will elicit a more favorable outcome. Either way, authority is deferring to influence.

This leads to our "on the other hand," which is this: although this Revelation goes a long way in identifying a Fox, it is also the most difficult for sellers to detect, for two reasons:

a. Of all the Revelations, this is the one that Foxes most want to keep invisible. As we cited in Chapter 4, there are practical reasons why powerful people work quietly behind the scenes while less skillful fighters engage in noisy, public confrontations. Such heavy-handedness comes at a price. Instead of being perceived as confident, others might see you as arrogant; instead of astute, cunning; instead of someone who works well with others, as someone who uses people. These perceptions are important, as they directly impact an individual's effectiveness, influence, and longevity within an organization.

b. The Fox's desire not to draw too much attention to his or her influence spreading across departmental lines leads to the second reason that this Revelation is difficult to identify: you can rarely observe it in real time. This is perhaps one of the most interesting, intriguing, and productive aspects of Fox Hunting. To see the interdepartmental exertion of influence, you often need to imagine it based on the results of the influence being applied. To be clear, this is not the same as fantasy. Here, imagination must serve to answer questions such as how people's thinking has changed, what decisions were made, or what actions have taken place. You can begin to see who might have been involved by looking at changes within the department onto which someone exerted influence. So put on your detective hat and sharpen your inductive skills as we launch into this most fascinating area of organizational politics. This is an area that is based on reverse engineering, an element of selling as a management science.

Simply put, Foxes often get involved in projects that are outside of their current job scope. They often will influence decisions before they are formally made, regardless of the department in which they originated. Foxes also have a large network and mentor high performers across multiple departments, while maintaining relationships with others who possess expertise beyond their own. Power Base members also build relationships beyond their department, largely in assistance to a Fox who may want to exert lateral influence across a subordinate level. Although individuals outside the Power Base certainly have cross-departmental relationships, they are generally not politically purposeful.

> ## FOX-HUNTING OBSERVATION
>
> Recognize that there may be no tangible relationship from one department to another in many situations where a sales opportunity exists—only a political one. Look for individuals who know what's going on in that department and are able to sway decisions there.

Let's look at an example of the potential for someone to exert influence across departmental lines and how it might impact a competitive sales situation. Suppose that a Marketing Department is considering purchasing a predictive analytics solution. They communicate to suppliers competing for the business, of which you are one, the well-defined decision-making criteria on which the decision will be based. They also explain that certain individuals within the Marketing Department have been assigned responsibility for the supplier evaluations. These decision makers will make a recommendation to the VP of Marketing when they are ready.

The VP of Marketing is a well-connected, politically astute, and business-savvy leader who has experienced the benefits of math modeling in past companies. However, she knows that she does not currently have people like those she's had in the past with the math skills necessary to make the solution successful. She is very aware that her department will need help, but she is not eager to make that known to everyone.

Based on your intel, you feel that the VP of Engineering could be in the Situational Power Base; he might even be the Fox, particularly if he is in the Enterprise Power Base. If you are right, the VP of Marketing will soon be contacting the VP of Engineering for assistance. Although she *could* approach an outside contractor for help, that would be very visible. You recognize this and proactively contact the VP of Engineering; you introduce yourself and your company and express your belief that you can significantly help Marketing succeed with the new analytics initiative. You also mention that you were contemplating the possibility of coordinating a joint effort with Engineering to provide the resident expertise necessary to ensure that success.

Your approach is exploratory, but the VP of Engineering takes it in the spirit intended, which helps to align you with him. You then wait and do what all the other competitors are doing; work with Marketing. However, there's one big difference in your approach; you have begun to build a relationship with a person who may be the Situational Fox. While your competitors focus on Marketing alone, your connection with Engineering may have given you the ability to shape the decision criteria and "ride" the Situational Fox's influence into Marketing.

The process begins as soon as the VP of Marketing contacts the VP of Engineering to discuss support. Even if this doesn't occur, you always have the option of suggesting that the Marketing VP leverage the Engineering group until she is able to build her organization, while also committing increased technical support from your company as an adjunct. In that regard, you are acting as a catalyst.

How do you know whether your hypothesis, that the VP of Engineering may be the Situational Fox, is correct? There are multiple ways this could play out. You may be fortunate enough to be in the right place at the right time and observe the VP of Engineering enter a meeting in which the VP of Marketing defers to him. Or, the VP of Engineering could send a delegate who shows up at certain key meetings and wields a great deal of power. And if you were not present at any of these meetings, what transpired can be conveyed to you as a result of good questioning.

However, for the reasons explained, such visible signs are not common when a Fox is exerting influence beyond his or her department. Instead, you need to look again at what has changed and why. This is where Foxes leave subtle traces of their activities, like fox prints in the snow.

For example, let's say that someone from Marketing begins asking a series of technical questions late in the sales cycle that were not part of the original buying criteria that had been communicated to you. It becomes clear when you politely ask a few clarifying questions that the Marketing person does not fully understand the technical concepts. This should indicate to you that someone else created the questions for this Marketing person to ask. Who could that be, and in what department might that person work?

The Marketing person might provide access to the expert source if you politely seek clarification. If that person is, in fact, in Engineering—and is someone with whom you can meet to better understand what is driving the questions—you could be getting closer to the Fox. Suppose you uncover that the technical direction that Engineering is establishing with Marketing aligns with the views that you know the VP of Engineering holds. Could the VP of Engineering be the Situational Fox? This type of induction, combined with other Revelations, will often give the answer. Again, back to reverse engineering.

This sales situation might evolve in many different ways. However, it's most critical for you to do the following:

- *Always look beyond the decision-making environment.* The Situational Power Base often extends into other departments.
- *Cover the bases.* Meet with people on an exploratory basis to determine whether there is the potential for them to become involved in a key decision or whether such a decision will impact them in some way.
- *Watch for connections.* Communication lines can illuminate the places where influence is exerted. If the VP of Marketing meets with the VP of Engineering, it strengthens the possibility that Engineering will be involved in the project and could therefore shape the buying process.
- *Consider becoming a catalyst.* If a business rationale exists for one department to become involved with another department, don't be shy about making a recommendation to that effect. But do be careful! Any intervention of this type needs to be:
  - Carefully thought out. Make certain that you're basing this on solid and impartial reasoning.
  - Professionally implemented. Communicate clearly and effectively; be positive, sincere, and respectful.
  - Politically nonintrusive. Never discuss anything political; stick to the business issues at hand.

Your ability to identify the potential for influence to cross from one department to another has significant implications. The previous example shows how many of your competitors would likely focus exclusively on Marketing and never make the possible connection to Engineering. It also clearly exhibits how gaining any kind of Political Advantage can potentially translate into relative superiority.

If you think traditionally, as Stage I or II sellers do by focusing only on the department where the sale is occurring, you limit your field of view within the account. To spot the extended reach of a Fox, you must sell well beyond the department of the sale, even though there are no decision makers present.

Now let's look at the Political Revelations—places where Foxes become somewhat visible from the standpoint of what motivates them or others around them. Figure 6.6 displays foxlike behaviors, along with recognition of their power and wisdom in the left-hand column, and shows the motivation that drives them in the center column. Finally, you can contrast this to Power Base members in the column to the right.

Figure 6.6
Political Revelations—Expanded

Foxes...	Because...	Power Base Members...
1) Help shape their organization's strategy, philosophy, and culture	They are committed to the success and well-being of their company	Are well-informed implementers; "in the know"
2) Tend to work on projects that are strategically important to their company's success	It maximizes their value to the company, while strengthening key relationships	Often are taken to "where the action is" by the Fox
3) Are often shown subtle acknowledgments of respect by others	Savvy people know the power and wisdom of the Fox	Opinions are sought out by the Fox; look to Fox for mentorship and advice
4) Are effective risk takers	They think like innovators and innovation always carries risk	Help to manage and reduce risk under direction of the Fox
5) Know how and when to appropriately and successfully work in exception to company policy	They are able to balance the intent of a policy with the value to be provided	Operate in exception to policy with Fox's approval
6) Have a history of exerting influence outside of their department, division, or business unit	Influence knows no boundaries	Go where the Fox's influence takes them

You are now ready to integrate and apply what we've discussed in this section—politics, influence and authority, Foxes, Power Base members, and how to measure influence—toward the ultimate goal of *gaining Political Advantage*. Simply put, how do you motivate Foxes and Power Base members to support you? This is the topic of our next chapter.

CHAPTER 7

GAINING POLITICAL ADVANTAGE

Recognition is the greatest motivator.

—Gerard C. Eakedale

Achieving Political Advantage requires that you motivate both Foxes and Power Base members to support you. It is their power that, when combined with value and strategy, produces a kind of synergy to disproportionately advance you to relative superiority. This means winning more business while also enhancing customer loyalty.

To accomplish this, we introduce two highly effective approaches to providing Power Base members with value. Both of these approaches go a long way toward enabling you to build good relationships with them. We then transition to a process that will allow you to divide those customer relationships into four distinct groups. Once all this in place, you'll be able to determine who is in the Power Base and distinguish the type of relationship that you have with them. Things become even more exciting when you add a competitor to the mix. In this step, you will create a graphic illustration of your actual competitive position from a political alignment point of view.

Building great Power Base relationships doesn't happen by accident, and it's not the outcome of hard work alone. You form these connections by learning the rules of the game. One such rule that resides at the epicenter of politics is what we call the Power Base Principle—and when you learn to leverage this, you can begin to provide Power Base members with value. To understand how this works in an actual sales scenario, we'll use a practical example that brings it to life.

THE POWER BASE PRINCIPLE

Let's look at an organization that is about to make a major buying decision connected with an important project. Ray Andrews, an ambitious and
young first-level manager, has been given responsibility to select a supplier.
Although final approval rests with Ray's boss, Beth McCullough, and the
division's Vice President, Chris Dalghren, the decision is primarily Ray's.
Figure 7.1 shows the organization chart. It's not necessary to go into the
details of this company or project; simply place your product and one of
your customers into the picture as we go along.

Figure 7.1
Ray Andrews on His Department Organization Chart

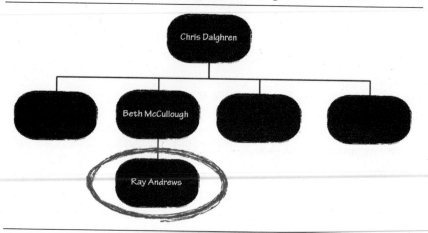

Ray begins by identifying which features and benefits that he feels the
product needs to have, and then he develops a list of suppliers who may
offer those capabilities. He then issues a request for proposal (RFP), and you
are one of the suppliers who respond to it. Fast-forward to the end of the
sales cycle. After a successful sales campaign, you win the order.

Since Ray's company is growing, Chris Dalghren is considering creating
a new department. Whoever she names to run it will be on the same level
as Beth McCullough. None of this is going to happen right away; it probably won't take place until a year or so down the line. Now, suppose that
Ray wants to be promoted to head the new department. Has he navigated
the political waters within his company in such a way that will help him
advance to that position? Let's take a look.

Ray has done a good job evaluating and selecting a supplier for the
project he has just completed. Has Ray significantly improved his chances

of being promoted as a result of his work alone? Of course, it would be nice if the answer were yes—and it sometimes is. Perhaps the answer is maybe. But the most politically astute answer is no.

We all know people who have worked hard their entire lives and done a good job, yet never seem to have gotten ahead. While *failing* to do a good job can get you fired, simply doing a good job never guarantees that a person will advance in an organization. Success requires something more.

Suppose Ray Andrews did more than a good job and brought something else to the table. He didn't just fulfill a directive; he saw the big picture and linked everything he did to the larger business issues his company is facing. For example, he looked beyond his own department to see whether he could learn from anyone who had dealt with similar issues or whether there were other needs he could fold into whatever solution he proposed. He worked with you, the supplier, to come up with a more innovative approach to his company's requirements than what an off-the-shelf solution would offer. He provided something special, both in the results of his efforts and the way he went about them. He provided *value*.

Now, knowing that Ray provided value to the organization, we ask again, will he get ahead? Unfortunately, the answer at this point is still no. In addition to hardworking people who are not moving up, there are those who provide real value but who have reached a premature plateau in their careers.

"Value" is only *one* component of a foundational tenet that the Power Base Principle addresses. It is a ticket that gets you into the theater, but it does not get you the seat you want. What else does Ray Andrews need to do in order to advance?

Ray can provide all the value in the world, but it doesn't mean anything if *the right people do not know about it*. That is why the second component of the Power Base Principle is *recognition*. In short:

Value and recognition go hand-in-hand.

Value plus recognition builds power. The right people must become aware of the value Ray represents, and in this case, the right people are members of senior management. Furthermore, the value Ray *believes* he represents must truly *be* of value to these right people—specifically, to Chris Dalghren. All the creative things Ray did to provide value will amount to very little if Chris does not recognize them as valuable or does not know that Ray was responsible for them.

Let's expand our story a bit by saying that all this has occurred. Chris Dalghren sees the way in which Ray goes about his task and the results he obtains as truly valuable, and she likes Ray's performance and approach. Now, is Ray going to get ahead? Has he substantially improved the odds of winning the promotion? The answer is yes. Of course, other factors will also be considered in the final decision, but Ray is well positioned for a favorable outcome. He must be fundamentally qualified for the job and may have to compete with other qualified candidates, but he has an advantage. Ray has taken the first step on a path defined by the Power Base Principle—realizing and acting according to the rule that:

VALUE + RECOGNITION = POWER

When value is recognized, it increases one's political influence or power. As soon as Chris Dalghren recognizes that Ray Andrews' approach and the results he obtained have contributed significant and possibly Unexpected Value, an informal bond begins to develop between the two. Ray now has an association with authority.

And who do you suppose Chris Dalghren will likely rely on as the organization faces new challenges? To whom will she delegate important matters? You guessed it: Ray Andrews. As she does this more frequently, the bond between Chris and Ray will become stronger and more visible, and it will manifest itself in a number of ways. For example, Chris might stop for a moment and chat with Ray in the cafeteria—something that she does not do with many other people. She may send Ray text messages when she wants a quick opinion or drop by Ray's office from time to time just to bounce a few ideas off him. As time goes on, Ray will have informal access to Chris, while his colleagues must still use more formal channels.

None of this interaction goes unnoticed by Ray's colleagues. While some of Ray's peers think that he is simply kissing up to the boss, others will be more astute and savvy. They will start to model their work behavior after Ray's, and the smart ones may even work to hitch their wagons to his star.

How does Beth McCullough, Ray's boss, feel as Ray's influence is building and his bond with Chris grows stronger? Just as with Ray's colleagues, it could go either way. Beth could be happy to see Ray's influence increase and feel that it was her success, too. Or she may view Ray's growing visibility as a diminution of her own and try to stop it. As Chris delegates a growing number of high-value projects to him, Ray's influence, political strength, and power will continue to increase. At some point, he will reach a stage where his influence is disproportionate to his authority.

If Ray continues to deliver value that others recognize, he will reach a point where management will increase his authority and promote him, as shown in Figure 7.2. At this point, something significant about the political dynamics of an organization should have become clear. An increase in Ray Andrews' authority *followed* his increased influence; therefore,

Increased influence often precedes increased authority.

This is an important fact to keep in mind about organizations. Many people believe (incorrectly, of course) that if they are promoted to the right position, they will finally get a chance to "do something." The reverse is actually true. Generally, one must first do something to get the position one wants—and that "something" that people must do is to apply the Power Base Principle in order to find ways to provide the right value—and make sure the right people know about it. Ray Andrews went out and defined his own role in this way, using the Power Base Principle.

Figure 7.2
Influence Disproportionate to Authority

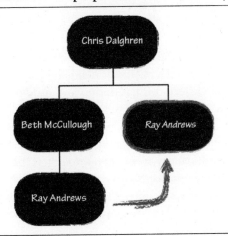

GAINING POLITICAL ADVANTAGE

Although this story is intended to deepen your understanding of how individuals gain influence, you may be wondering what it has to do with your ability as a seller to gain Political Advantage. The answer is, a lot. What role did you, a supplier, play in Ray's promotion in this example? Although you did have a role in this story, it was a bit part, a cameo appearance with a good product. You won the order because you sold well, in a traditional sense. Your product worked well, and its success launched Ray on a path to success. This initial opportunity to provide value and be recognized for it then led to other opportunities and other successes. Eventually, Ray won a coveted position. And although all these things happened, you did not *make* them happen.

Come to think of it, the way we told the story, Ray Andrews seems like a pretty remarkable person. He knew how to approach the project in a way that senior management would most highly value. He knew that his company was likely to create the new department soon and that succeeding in the project would give him a shot at the new position.

But what if Ray was not so politically astute? What if he wasn't aware of what was going on in the organization? What if he did not have a read on Chris Dalghren's values? What if he did not realize that his buying decision represented more than simply selecting a product and was actually his first crack at becoming a member of the Power Base?

Is there a way for you, the seller, to fill this void—and as a result, gain a tremendous Political Advantage? Yes, there is; and it is actually your *job* to do so. Stage IV Customer Advisors make the Power Base Principle work for them by making it work for one of their customers like Ray Andrews. Customer Advisors provide indirect political support to customer Foxes, Power Base members, and those people who have the potential to become part of the Power Base. This not only helps the people involved but also improves the overall customer organization and simultaneously strengthens your relationship with the Power Base.

But the process doesn't stop here. Individuals seek other aspirations that they consider important—and these aspirations provide Stage IV Customer Advisors with an opportunity to further strengthen their relationship with customer individuals. These aspirations are what we call *Personal Motivators,* and advancing them is the second and most powerful way you can add value to Power Base members.

PERSONAL MOTIVATORS

A Personal Motivator is what an individual wants to achieve as a result of the value he or she brings to his or her organization. Note that the "value to the organization" is a critical element of this.

We've seen many Personal Motivators from the competitive deals we've coached and have noticed that most of the time, three common and distinct categories emerge. These are summarized in Figure 7.3.

Figure 7.3
Three Categories of Personal Motivators

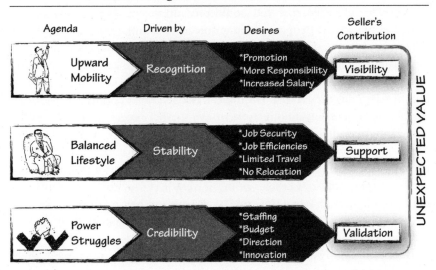

The first is *upward mobility*. Many influential people want to advance their careers and be promoted. Indeed, this is what motivated Ray Andrews. These people are likely striving for more organizational stature, responsibility, and money. As the Power Base Principle outlines, this becomes possible when other people recognize their value. Therefore, sellers need to help these individuals gain recognition and visibility. For example, perhaps a customer Power Base member is seeking to raise her public profile in order to support her being considered for an executive role at her company. A valuable seller might help secure her a public speaking opportunity at an industry conference.

A second category of Personal Motivators is *balanced lifestyle*. These are individuals who are motivated less by career advancement and more by life experience. For example, they may wish to travel or not, to relocate to a certain place or stay where they are. This Personal Motivator could be permanent or temporary. Although they do tend to be longer-term oriented, they can, of course, change and, at times, might reflect a short-term goal that someone has internalized.

An example is an individual who has prioritized upward mobility in the past, putting in long hours for the company, but now wants to (temporarily) spend less time in the office. Perhaps he needs to care for a sick parent or spend more time with a child about to leave home for college. People who are motivated in this way often seek job security and efficiencies. Suppose, for example, that you could provide the customer with specific resources or support people to help ensure success and reduce the workload for the key person, thus advancing his or her Personal Motivator.

A third category of Personal Motivators that we see centers on winning *Power Struggles;* in other words, individuals who are competing with one another. Perhaps they're contending for budget, head count, control of an important project, setting direction, or some other objective. These healthy and natural conflicts are usually played out transparently, with individuals keeping the company's best interests in mind. For a seller, this represents an opportunity to provide third-party validation in terms of credibility and evidence that support a certain point of view. Let's say that your customer contact has an important meeting with one of her executives. Perhaps you could provide additional research, reports, and support to make her recommendation more substantive.

In addition to the specific areas of contribution just mentioned, there is one opportunity to advance all the Personal Motivators that we have discussed, and that is by providing *Unexpected Value* to the customer. For example, Unexpected Value will significantly advance upward mobility, differentiating a candidate from others seeking the same position. In the area of balanced lifestyle, an exception to company policy may be necessary, which requires extraordinary value to the company as justification. And lastly, winning a Power Struggle requires relative superiority, and the best source of that superiority is Unexpected Value.

As a result, this is where a powerful connection takes place between providing Unexpected Value to the customer and advancing the Personal Motivator of a Power Base member. When this occurs, you often achieve a decisive advantage over the competition; in other words, you achieve relative superiority.

As with identifying influence, the process of uncovering Personal Motivators relies on insight gained from your intel gathering. Again, you do this through customer research, astute observations, and good questions. The word *personal* should tell you that these are usually desires that individuals do not want to broadcast publicly—which brings us to two points:

1. Conversations that provide insight into Personal Motivators are best conducted within informal settings.
2. Personal Motivators are aspirations that people have taken to heart and internalized. As a result, you conceptually "attach" yourself to that motivator when you advance it. You become internalized—that is, personally and professionally significant to the customer individual.

UNCOVERING AND ADVANCING PERSONAL MOTIVATORS

The ability to uncover and advance Foxes' and Power Base members' Personal Motivators is a powerful source of Political Advantage. Of course, you can't possibly do this unless you're providing strong business value to their organization that is linked to a Personal Motivator, as previously explained. What we are talking about is the ability to provide political and cultural value *in addition to and not in place of* product and business value. We address this Unexpected Value in more detail in the next section of the book; for now, let's discuss how to uncover and advance Personal Motivators.

We use a scenario that illustrates the three steps summarized in Figure 7.4.

Figure 7.4
Uncovering Personal Motivators

Intelligence	Personal Motivator	Confirmation
-Customer Research -Astute Observations -Insightful Questions	Formulate Hypothesis	Determine Potential Contribution and Test Hypothesis

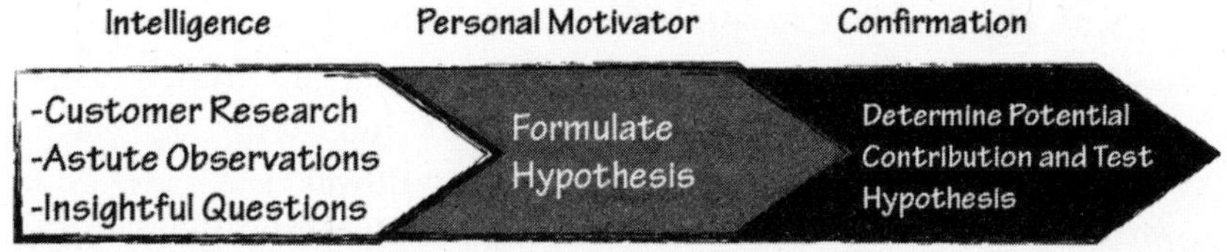

Let's touch on an example that is close to home for sellers—one that concerns an up-and-coming telecommunications provider that wanted to increase its share of large enterprise business, which largely meant taking it from their competition. This company's Chief Executive Officer (CEO) realized that his sales organization needed new thinking and new leadership in order to live up to its potential. Before long, he made an announcement identifying a new Vice President (VP) of Sales—a man named Jeff Gahagan, who had a reputation for building world-class sales organizations that out-performed competitors and who could hit the street running.

Jeff restructured the sales force to create an enterprise sales group composed of business developers. Their job was to penetrate and develop new accounts while also building competitive immunity into existing ones, thereby protecting and growing the installed base. However, Jeff knew that these business developers needed to be very consultative and innovative in creating customer solutions to accomplish this. Jeff had succeeded in the past not just by building and managing sales organizations well, but by the way in which the rest of the company adapted to his actions and initiatives. Although his company would still offer "cookie cutter" or prepackaged solutions, they'd also make a new level of customization available. That meant enacting changes in their Design, Engineering, Manufacturing, Support, and Marketing Departments if they were truly going to put customers' needs first.

History had taught Jeff that the right market segments would reward this type of quality with increased revenue, margins, and customer satisfaction ratings. He also knew that if his approach succeeded, his competition would have a difficult time replicating it. His competitors were just too big, too set in their ways, and too accustomed to having customers adapt to *them*. Jeff's company had to build new infrastructure anyway, so why not do it right? This meant that Jeff needed to do two things:

1. Gain the support of what we would call the Enterprise Fox, the CEO in this case, and the VPs of Engineering and Manufacturing, both of whom were members of the Enterprise Power Base along with Jeff himself. Changing the way the other departments thought about the business and introducing new customer-centric practices would be a challenge, but Jeff knew that if he had the right Power Base support, he could pull it off.

2. Elevate the business development (BD) team within the company, which is critical for two reasons: First, BD managers must form relationships with customer executives in order to develop solutions that will advance their business priorities and vision. Second, they needed to have significant influence internally to drive customer initiatives forward. Therefore, Jeff did something nontraditional to provide this influence; he eliminated two levels of reporting above the BD managers, thereby structuring the organization so that the BD team now reported directly to him. This meant that Jeff would

be intimately familiar with every single enterprise account from a strategy perspective. And because his BD managers each had director level status and pay, the customer quickly became a true priority for the company.

Part of the new infrastructure included selecting and deploying a Customer Relationship Management (CRM) system to support account planning, manage the pipeline, forecast sales, and provide an array of leading indicator metrics that would help proactively manage sales campaigns. It was not, however, to overburden the field with needless reporting. Jeff understood the difference between these efforts; he knew what he wanted and how to make it work. Still, he decided to conduct an evaluation to select the right supplier.

This is where you come in, as one of the suppliers. It doesn't take long for you to launch your Fox-Hunting activities and determine that Jeff is the Situational Fox. You also uncover during your intel gathering that Jeff spent several months very early on traveling to all the company's facilities to understand their local markets. He personally met with noncompetitive industry leaders to better understand their approach to growing their enterprise businesses. He also spent a great deal of time searching for best practices to add to his own, while beginning to build a reputation for innovative sales management.

Over time, the sales cycle progressed and you were down selected to the short list. Soon it was between you and one other supplier, both of you from good companies and proposing effective solutions. Next, you moved into the hypothesize phase for determining Jeff's Personal Motivator. Although you would have liked to get there sooner, you knew that the more obvious Personal Motivator of simply creating the expected success for his company was not enough to distinguish you from the competition. You knew that Jeff wanted more, but what was it?

The hypothesis began to take shape when you observed that Jeff spent a lot of time with industry analysts, leaders, and members of the press. You postulated that his goal was to achieve strong personal recognition at the industry and country level. Whether this was to gain recognition for its own sake, to set himself up for a CEO position in the future, to pave the way to starting his own consulting firm, or for some other reason, you simply didn't know. But you were fairly sure that he was on the road to making a name for himself in the world of business development, beyond the field of telecommunications.

The only thing left to do was to test the hypothesis. If you had it right, there would still be time to enhance your proposal in such a way as to advance Jeff's Personal Motivator—if your competitor didn't get there first. With a real sense of urgency, you would meet with Jeff and wait for a casual moment to present your thoughts: "Jeff, not to be overconfident or presumptuous, but I have been speaking with our Marketing Department and we are very excited about the innovative thinking and practices that you are establishing to grow enterprise market share. Assuming that we work together, would you be interested in speaking at our telecommunications conference next year and participating in a joint article that we are preparing for a leading business publication? We are excited to be part of your team and believe that there would be a lot of interest in the best practices that you're implementing."

Generally speaking, the response to this type of test is binary. Because the individual has internalized his or her Personal Motivator and considers it important, the reaction will be visibly positive or absolutely neutral. Jeff's enthusiasm and unhesitating agreement in this case told you that you were on to something. As such, you offer to set up a meeting with your VP of Marketing at corporate and, following that, organize a lunch with your CEO. All of this looks to be part of a supplier evaluation process to everyone else, since a supplier decision has not yet been made. However, you know that similar meetings with your competition are not taking place.

You soon find out that you have been selected. You know that you have outsold your competition, but how, exactly? Both companies had good solutions, were committed to the customer's success, and were credible providers. But you had an advantage—*Political Advantage!*

BUILDING INFLUENTIAL RELATIONSHIPS

Building relationships with influential people begins by knowing what kind of relationships you want to build. At the end of the day, the value that you provide to individuals at both the business and personal levels, all that you have in common with them and your level of compatibility in terms of operating principles, will result in the development of a certain type of relationship. That doesn't mean that everyone is going to like you; however, it does suggest that defeating your competition will be like rolling a big rock uphill if you get the relationships wrong—possible, but never fun and *always* exhausting.

Figure 7.5
Don't Rely on Santa's "Nice List" to Characterize Your Relationships

Consistent with their belief in sales as a management science, Stage IV Customer Advisors have a process and method for characterizing customer relationships. As Figure 7.5 playfully suggests, they do not leave it up to chance or luck.

So, let's take a look at the five types of relationships that will populate your account landscape, as depicted in Figure 7.6, from most to least desirable.

Figure 7.6
Five Types of Relationships

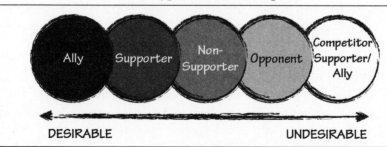

1. **The Ally** is a strong advocate, committed to you and your company's current and future success. He or she proactively assists you in any way possible, such as introducing you to customer executives and providing you with relevant insight, principally because you have already proved your value. An Ally wants you to succeed long term in the account by winning multiple deals and will often draft you into new accounts when he or she moves to new companies. Allies also are your best references, since they're known for proactively contacting companies when asked to do so by the seller.

2. **The Supporter** is committed to helping you win a specific opportunity. Some Supporters are *passive,* sharing information with you and coaching you along the way. Others are *active,* publicly endorsing your solution and willing to take on risk to help you succeed. Supporters within a Power Base are more likely to be active than passive, given the general nature of Power Base members.

3. **The Non-Supporter** is neutral; he or she is usually new to the group, not very involved, not interested, or simply undecided.

4. **The Opponent** is an individual who actively does *not* support you. However, this is not because Opponents support the competition; those would be Competitor Supporters or Allies. Instead, an Opponent contradicts you because:

   - You are aligned with an individual who is engaged in a Power Struggle. This is always the risk of supporting one person in this kind of situation. The individual at the other end of the Power Struggle will inherently become an Opponent—someone who can easily evolve to a Competitor Supporter if the situation allows for it.

   - He or she has an ax to grind with your company. Perhaps this person recommended a competitor in a past supplier evaluation and was overruled. Or, maybe this person was involved in a bad installation by your company, which reflected negatively on him or her.

   - The person opposes the company initiative that has resulted in a supplier evaluation. For this individual, failure to make a decision is a victory.

   - The Opponent is part of an in-house group that should be doing what a supplier is proposing to do. As a result, the in-house group's credibility will be damaged, and jobs may be lost.

5. **The Competitor Supporter or Ally** is committed to helping your competitor win either a specific opportunity if a Supporter or longer-term success if an Ally.

Personal compatibility and shared values play a role in building relationships, as does the customer's disposition, which is something you can influence. People will be more inclined to support you if:

- *You are willing to invest in them.* Take time to understand people; learn their likes and dislikes, what excites or worries them, what they consider important in how they work—and, above all, what matters most to them. This certainly takes time, which is why it is so important to go Fox Hunting first. You cannot afford to invest in the wrong people. It's fun to work with people you like or who appreciate what you do, and it's fine to do that within accounts occasionally. But you want to spend most of your time and effort focusing on building powerful Supporters and Allies.

- *You are willing to invest in the account.* Spend time attempting to really understand how the customer's organization is structured and what the business priorities and strategic concerns are. Determine the markets in which it operates and its competitive position within those markets, as well as its history and future plans. Figure out how technology, competition, or other specific trends are impacting and will continue to impact its business. This takes time also, which is one of the reasons that qualifying accounts and opportunities is always important.

- *You are willing to invest in the solution to addressing the customer's needs.* This is where caring more about the customer than the competition becomes most important. If you don't show concern for the customer's situation and needs, you're selling like a Stage I commodity provider and not a solutions provider—and people will sense this. It's not necessarily about committing resources or discounting or always saying "yes." It is about making an emotional commitment.

Although you're now ready to build relationships, it's going to take some time. You can't establish trust with others overnight, so be patient. Most sellers are drivers, so achieving this sense of trust can be difficult. You must be willing to stay the course and make the investment.

There is a lot more to say about building relationships, but this approach will get you there most of the time. It's also a process that lends itself to teamwork, as you will inevitably include others in some of the bigger accounts. These people need to work in lockstep with your relationship-building activities.

ASSESSING RELATIONSHIP TYPE

You will need to determine how you are doing as you build these relationships. You must also monitor your competition in terms of the relationships that *they* are building. To help you do so, you can apply the following guide to yourself and your competition. It is intended to provide directionally correct insight into the type of relationships that you and others form.

Let's take a look at characteristics of each that will emerge if you invest in building these relationships:

1. **Allies**
   - Will provide you with more insight into the account and sales situation.
   - If you really care about these people and they are in turn compassionate people, will begin to care about you. But what if they are not? In that case, they would likely not become Allies but might still become Supporters.
   - Will be open (to a degree) to discussing their Personal Motivators.
   - Will provide you with direction that will help you uncover other sales opportunities within the account and will introduce you to helpful customer individuals.
   - Will actively support both your solution and your company.
2. **Supporters**
   - Will often be somewhat open to discussing their Personal Motivators.
   - Will often be more supportive of your solution than your company.
3. **Non-Supporters**
   - This relationship category is quite straightforward, except when you have an Opponent who is masquerading as a Non-Supporter. This individual will seem to be neutral but is secretly doing everything possible to derail your sales campaign. The best way to uncover this is by talking to other customer individuals who may be in or out of the Power Base. Don't expect them to volunteer any information, however; you must ask questions to gain the necessary insight, as we discussed in terms of intel gathering.
4. **Opponents**
   - Will, like Allies, generally be active in nature—except that they're negative instead of positive.
   - Will openly express and make their views known. However, when you do break through, if at all, they tend to become Allies, not Supporters.

- Will often respond to a direct approach. Give them a chance to vent, express their views, and say whatever else they need to get off their chest. Accept, listen, and don't react or argue.
- Will be a challenge. Although it is easy to care for nice people, it is a bear to really care for difficult people. It's therefore quite admirable if you can muster up some compassion for your Opponents, since real caring is always seen in the face of adversity.
- Should be made your highest relationship priority—and move quickly! Although this may sound counterintuitive, it is imperative for two reasons: First, Opponents often act as "magnets" to your competition, and you want to fend off conversion to a Competitor Supporter. Second, Opponents can be highly destructive to your sales campaign.

5. **Competitor Supporters or Allies**
   - Will display the same characteristics as previously described for Supporters and Allies; however, they direct their help toward your competitor.
   - Should be dealt with indirectly. Unlike the recommended direct approach with Opponents, the influence required to contain or alter a Competitor Supporter's views must come from within the customer organization.

Now, let's merge political and relationship information to form a picture that will speak volumes in terms of insight. At a glance, it will graphically depict whether you or your competitor has relative superiority in a sales situation. Remember: if you have it, you win. Without it, you lose; it's as simple as that.

CREATING A SUPPORT BASE MAP

Figure 7.7 displays a multi-dimensional picture that conveys information about influence and relationship type. The center depicts the Fox by his or her name, which, in this example, is Chris. If you move concentrically outward, you find people in the Power Base, such as in our example, Tim and Ray, whereas individuals in the outer white ring are considered outside of the Power Base. Superimposed on this is the type of relationships that you—or your competitors—have with specific people, just as we talked about earlier. In this example, Ray is in the Power Base and is a Supporter of yours. Tim, who is also in the Power Base, supports your competitor, shown by the triangle.

Figure 7.7
Support Base Map

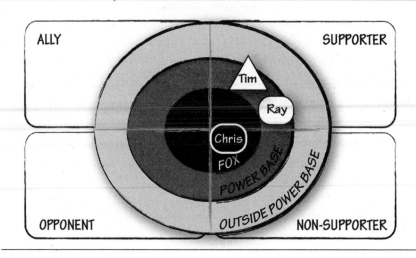

Political Advantage and Value Creation, in terms of Unexpected Value, are about building relative superiority, as reflected in your Support Base. It compels you to ensure that Foxes and Power Base members are Allies and Supporters and to always keep a vigilant eye on the competition. Remember: a *Situational Power Base* is dynamic and fluid. The appearance of an Emerging Fox can signal overnight change. Recognizing this, Stage IV sellers track the progression of relationships within their accounts, as well as that of their competition. They try not to be caught off guard or surprised by shifts in the political landscape or new relationships that might be forming. It all comes down to one question: Who has or will have the relative superiority necessary to win the business?

POLITICAL IMPLICATIONS

Figure 7.7 populates your Support Base Map using our Ray Andrews example from earlier in this chapter. Suppose that a few months have passed; the original product that you sold to Ray's company is performing well, and the customer is pleased. Now Ray is considering you for a new opportunity, involving another of your products. You have determined that Chris Dalghren is the Situational Fox and is currently a Non-Supporter in this particular deal. Ray Andrews is in Chris's Power Base and is a Supporter. However, a customer individual named Tim Colby is also in Chris's Power Base, but he supports your competitor, as shown by the triangle.

What does this tell you? That you must get to Chris before the competition does. And you can accomplish this by leveraging your relationship with Ray, who is in the Power Base. You will need him to sponsor you to Chris, who is the Fox. You will also need insight into what might be Chris's Personal Motivator, along with her vision, direction, and priorities for the group. You want Chris to become your Supporter before the competition can get to her.

Now, put yourself in the competition's shoes; what would you do if you were them? You would take the same approach, but with Tim. Since he is in the Power Base, he by definition has access to Chris as well. If you and your competitor are taking the same approach, what will enable you to build relative superiority ahead of your competitor? Our deal experience highlights two factors that are critical:

1. *Time:* Whoever gets to the Fox first has a tremendous advantage. That's why it is so crucial to construct a Support Base Map early in a sales campaign and keep it current.
2. *Your ability to use the time you have to develop whatever insight you can into the Fox's Personal Motivator:* This is where selling from the hip leaves off and selling as a management science begins.

Now, let's go back in time a bit. Suppose that you identified that Ray was in the Situational Power Base, that you developed a pretty good handle on his Personal Motivator, and that you positioned yourself to advance it. Remember, Ray wanted to be promoted. If he had then become an Ally, when would you have likely learned about the new opportunity relative to your competition? Probably sooner. When might you have gotten access to Chris through Ray, relative to the competition? Again, probably sooner.

Therefore, this type of relative superiority is a function of:

- *Political Advantage,* which is determined by the types of relationships that you have with people and how much power or influence those individuals possess.
- *Timing,* which requires that you build your Support Base Map *early* in the sales cycle, as it will shape the trajectory of your sales campaign.

In the next chapter, we explore, in more depth, unexpected and competitively differentiated value and how it contributes to relative superiority. We will move up the customer's value chain, working to exceed expectations while utilizing Political Advantage to assist us in the process.

PART 3

UNEXPECTED VALUE

CHAPTER 8

MOVING UP THE SALES VALUE CHAIN

Now my eyes are turned from the South to the North, and I want to lead one more expedition. This will be the last . . . to the North Pole.
—Sir Ernest Shackleton

A company's value chain is a concept that has been around for a long time. As businesses use a series of steps to manufacture products, each step adds new value. At the end, the finished product has a total value that should exceed the individual value added at each step along the way. This creates a value chain. But how does this relate to selling?

Traditional Stage I and II selling actually do not involve the value chain. During these stages, sellers work to understand what the customer needs, configure a solution, sell the value of the solution to secure the order, and then install it. No real process exists that continually adds value over time. Sometimes, customers know exactly what they want. On other occasions, it is difficult to change or submit an alternative solution once sellers submit a proposal. Buyers evaluate each supplier approach against criteria that will lead to a short list and then select a single supplier. It all makes sense, as customers try very hard to fairly judge each proposed solution's merits.

Or, does it?

Taking a nontraditional perspective, we ask: Why shouldn't a proposed solution improve in its value to the customer just as products improve during their production cycle?

Well, for one thing, products in discrete manufacturing are often made of subassemblies that were made of components formed from raw materials. There is a clear mechanical progression in the product's size, function, and value. If we can move up in the customer's organization in selling—building more and more insight as we go—is there a way to dramatically improve the impact of a proposed solution? Can we take an approach that would allow sellers to provide the customer with Unexpected Value that the customer did *not* know was possible?

What we are looking at is not the size and function of a solution, so much as the value and true cost of ownership of a solution. Everything will fall under these two solution elements, including:

- Solution functionality
- Installation and integration
- Supplier support capabilities
- Solution ease of use
- Internal labor requirements
- Potentially necessary internal process changes
- Direct and indirect costs to acquire, support, and maintain a solution

So—does the value chain concept apply to customer solutions? The answer is yes, but not in terms of building a product. Instead, increases in value to the customer come from adapting a solution to certain customer factors in order to produce an extended significance. These factors will vary from company to company, division to division, and department to department. Each will have some kind of a vision and plan for realizing the vision, along with priorities and initiatives. There will be a set of factors at the departmental level, where acquisitions are likely to be made; the division or business unit level; and the corporate executive level. This cascading produces an extended significance, as shown in Figure 8.1, that maps a solution into customer priorities at multiple levels.

Figure 8.1
Sales Value Chain

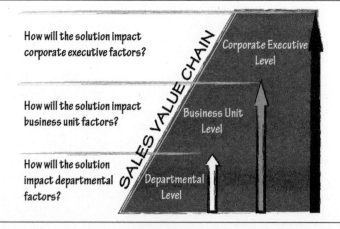

> This is a Sales Value Chain driven by two things: customer knowledge and solution flexibility.

Remember that the factors to which we are referring are rooted in each level's vision, business plan, and key initiatives. Understanding these factors and then adapting or modifying your solution to advance them at multiple customer levels is what creates a Sales Value Chain.

Let's go back to our telecommunications customer in Chapter 7. You will recall that the Vice President (VP) of Sales, Jeff Gahagan, needed to acquire a Customer Relationship Management (CRM) system to support his team of business developers, who had to increase enterprise market share. You won that business as the seller; however, look at what might have happened from a customer value point of view.

> A Sales Value Chain exists when your solution maps into two or more customer levels.

To accommodate each level of impact, you will likely modify your solution, adding customer value to each level. This creates an organizational view of your solution from operations up to the executive ranks. This, in turn, creates a perception of your company that is far greater than that which any one product or one-level solution could create. It also produces a customer executive perception of your company that is strategically value-centric versus product-centric.

For example, two levels were involved in the case of our CRM acquisition. First was the enterprise sales group, and second was the corporate executive level, specifically the Finance Department. Every supplier bidding on the business at the sales level focused on the identified CRM requirements, and each proposed solutions that provided similar value. You, however, were the only supplier to move north in the account in order to find a possible corporate executive sponsor.

As it turned out, the VP of Finance was instrumental in launching cost reduction initiatives across the company. This knowledge allowed you to tie your CRM solution to reducing cost of sales. In the enterprise space, sales campaigns can be quite costly, and with an approximate 30 percent hit rate, two-thirds of the pursuits returned no revenue for the effort. By deploying objective criteria for qualifying sales opportunities, using the CRM, and tying the result to a bid and proposal budget for each opportunity—approved by sales management and Finance—you knew that cost of sales would go down while the win rate would increase. The impact on expense and revenue would be impressive.

As such, you positioned your solution to do a good job for the enterprise sales group while also providing an extended significance to the Finance Department and thereby advancing the VP of Finance's priority. By moving up the Sales Value Chain, you promised, and ultimately delivered, Unexpected Value to the customer while differentiating yourself from the competition.

You may also recall that the total value of a finished product exceeded the sum of the value added at each stage of production in manufacturing. The same is true with the Sales Value Chain. By advancing a priority at the corporate executive level, you developed access to the Enterprise Power Base, a powerful group of people within an account. As such, your solution had not only extended significance to the customer but also extended significance to you in accelerating your development of the account.

And the benefit doesn't stop there. You also assisted Jeff Gahagan, whose CRM initiative is now directly advancing a corporate priority. This places you on a journey that will likely lead you down a path to becoming a Stage IV Customer Advisor in this customer's eyes. It is reflective of understanding that one solution may have many points of extended significance, moving it well up the Sales Value Chain.

MOVING NORTH

The importance of moving north in an account, to move up the Sales Value Chain, is emphasized when you look at a competitive sales opportunity. Think about an important and competitive deal that you are working on—a "must-win." Make a list of the most significant reasons why customers buy from your company. Now, look at the list you just created, crossing out anything that your competition could also say is a reason that customers would buy from *them*. For example, if you wrote down that you're "reliable," but your competitor can also claim reliability, cross it out. If you included a certain capability that your competition also has, then cross it out. Now look at the list again. How many of the reasons remain?

Next, go back and look at the original list of reasons. Circle the ones that you know your customer's Situational Power Base recognizes and accepts. For example, say you wrote down "high throughput"; does anyone in the Situational Power Base believe this to be true? If yes, circle it. If no, do not.

How many of the reasons listed are circled and do not have a line through them? This makes clear the nature and extent of Competitive Differentiation that you have, as viewed by the Situational Power Base. Our deal experience confirms that your value must be:

- Differentiated from the competition.
- Recognized and accepted by the customer's Power Base.

In the absence of an acknowledged and relevant difference between you and your competition, what will happen next? Making it onto a short list gives the customer's Procurement Department leverage to drive down price—and with that, down go your margins. On the other hand, if you move north—up the Sales Value Chain—value and Competitive Differentiation both increase. This, in turn, drives elasticity of demand, enabling you to protect and grow margins. Just as important, it helps ensure the win.

EXPANDING THE SALES VALUE CHAIN

We have talked about mapping a solution into the priorities that exist at multiple levels within a customer's organization. Now, let's build on that and do so within the context of the Holden Four Stage Model that we presented in Chapter 2.

Figure 8.2
Four Types of Value

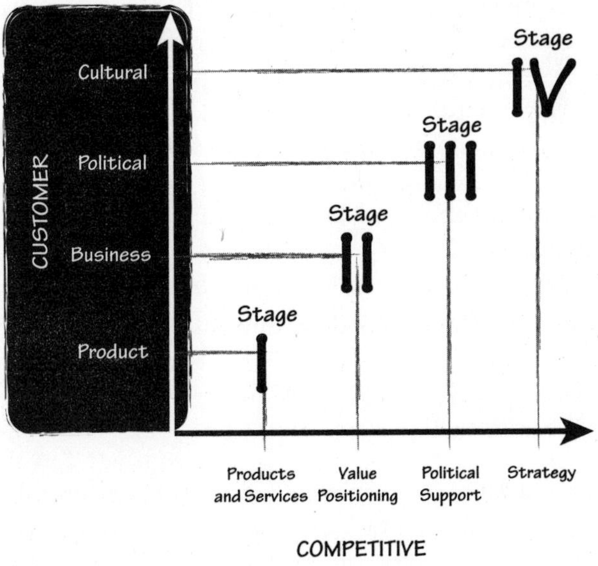

Figure 8.2 shows that there are really four stages or types of value that constitute the full Sales Value Chain. They center on:

1. **Product** being sold, often expressed in terms of features and benefits.
2. **Business** value, expressed in terms of value and total cost of ownership (TCO), based on linking or mapping into the priorities at multiple customer levels, as we have discussed.
3. **Political** value, generally expressed in terms of leveraging the Power Base Principle and advancing an individual's Personal Motivator.
4. **Cultural** value, which is often referred to in terms of accepted business norms or behavior within an organization. This impacts how you generate value. If someone produces value in an unacceptable manner, other members of the organization, particularly Foxes, will likely discount the value.

What value do customers expect, and what is unexpected? Why does this matter? To answer these questions, we look at this dimension of value in more depth.

EXPECTED VERSUS UNEXPECTED VALUE

There is an emotional component behind the intellectual recognition and appreciation of value. What makes a proposal engaging and exciting for a customer? Expected value is not exciting; it is required. But a positive emotion is often evoked when a person is not expecting something and it is a surprise. Look at it another way: What would be required for you to be promoted to a certain position? Three factors often make the difference:

1. A fundamental ability to do the job (just like meeting a customer's requirements)
2. A history of providing Unexpected Value that differentiates you from the competition (akin to moving up the Sales Value Chain with a customer)
3. Being recognized by a Fox (which you also want during a competitive sales campaign)

Supporters and Allies are established most quickly in any sales campaign when you provide them with Unexpected Value that prompts positive emotion. These feelings then motivate people to take action on your behalf. Think about it: even during something as simple as a sales call, it is not merely what you say, or think the customer heard, that counts. It is how he or she feels about the interaction and whether it produces excitement or ambivalence. This is why it is critical to move up the Sales Value Chain and transition from providing expected value to Unexpected Value.

Customers *expect* sellers to provide certain types of value, starting with Stage I *product value*. Regardless of how many Foxes you identify, Power Bases you map, and Personal Motivators you advance, you are unlikely to make a sale if you cannot fundamentally prove that your product meets the customer's requirements. This does not mean that you have to be an expert on every aspect of the product. But it does suggest that you must ensure that your customer understands and believes that your product meets the company's requirements during a sales cycle. This is where sales support, product specialists, online or onsite demonstrations, and marketing activities play a critical role.

Having said that, the Relevance Revolution, described in Chapter 1, established that although customers expect product value, this alone is not sufficient to ensure seller relevance to customers in today's world. Customers want *more* than product value. *Business* value is provided at a Stage II, which can be significant to the customer and seller if the seller moves up the Sales Value Chain, adding more value at each customer level. This is the point when you transition to providing Unexpected Value, as most sellers tend to stay at the lower part of the Sales Value Chain from a business value perspective. Simply stated, most sellers do not sell high enough and therefore do not create a multi-level customer solution.

Stage III sellers provide unexpected *political* value, as the vast majority of sellers have little awareness and ability to configure a solution in such a way as to advance a Power Base member's Personal Motivator. More specifically, you are not only advancing an individual's Personal Motivator; you are doing so by providing unexpected business value. As such:

Business value becomes connected to political value.

Because you are moving up the Sales Value Chain in a manner that provides the customer with unanticipated value, while differentiating yourself from the competition, you end up producing a powerful nontraditional source of relative superiority.

Stage IV Customer Advisors drive up this superiority even further. They know that by generating business and political value in a manner that is consistent with an organization's norms, values, and beliefs, they can maximize the total value perception. Suppose that the Fox believes that collaboration and teamwork are essential in approaching initiatives. Would it make sense to configure a solution or install it *without* a team that included your support people and the right customer individuals? Or perhaps a Fox sees leading-edge technology as critical to his or her company's success. You would obviously connect your R&D people with the Fox to lay out future technology development plans under a nondisclosure agreement. You must personify whatever defines the customer's culture in all that you do—the more, the better. The more you visibly align with and support it, the more a customer will value your solution.

We have talked about the customer knowledge and solution flexibility necessary to produce solutions that map into customer business priorities at multiple levels, as well as advancing Personal Motivators of Power Base members—and doing all this in a manner that aligns with customer culture. The result is moving up on the Sales Value Chain, where *how* Customer Advisors sell increases the value of *what* they sell. This suggests that many facets of value could characterize a customer solution. But not all of these aspects of value will be relevant to any one customer level, department, or individual. That is why in the next chapter we dive into the mechanics of moving up the Sales Value Chain.

CHAPTER 9

BUILDING EXPRESSIONS OF CUSTOMER VALUE

Make no little plans; they have no magic to stir men's blood.
—Daniel H. Burnham

You are now ready to learn to apply the Sales Value Chain to a specific customer organization. This chapter begins with a discussion about how to make value relevant depending on with whom in a customer organization you are working. From there, we will present two powerful value expressions—one qualitative and the other quantitative—that enable you to package business and political value in a way that creates relative superiority.

VALUE RELEVANCE

Not all these aspects of value will be relevant to any one particular customer individual. Before we dive into packaging expressions of value to move up the Sales Value Chain, we need to first determine what is relevant and to whom.

Customers measure value differently based on their role and responsibility within an organization. What is of interest to one person may not be important to another. To get a handle on this, let us look at a company structure as a pyramid. At the top are executives (E), in the middle is management (M), and forming the foundation is operations (O). We label this pyramid the E-M-O Model, as you can see in Figure 9.1.

Figure 9.1
The E-M-O Model of Value Relevance

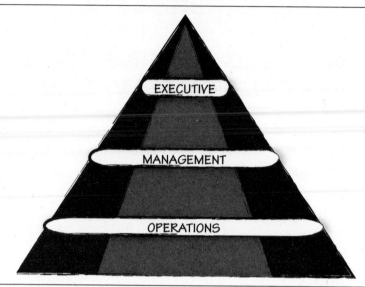

Characterizing an organization in terms of levels is not new. In fact, we already looked at the departmental, business unit, and executive levels as they relate to the Sales Value Chain earlier in the book. However, it is helpful to consider where individuals reside within the company hierarchy to get a better sense of how people think and act, what is important to them, and how they might view solution value.

Executive Value

Starting at the top of the pyramid, *executives* set the organization's mission, create a vision for success, and oversee every major function in the business, such as production, finance, sales, marketing, engineering, information technology (IT), and human resources (HR). They have a panoramic view from the top.

When considering or approving a particular supplier, executives base their view on how a solution will affect the fundamentals of the business: revenue, profit, market share, customer satisfaction, strategic investments, earnings per share, and so on.

Executives consider how a solution will better position them in the future relative to the business fundamentals they consider important. As such, they tend to be future-focused; they want to construct a specific vision for the company that provides employees, customers, investors, and industry analysts with a picture of what the company will look like years from that point. There is nothing more important to boosting employee morale than giving people a sense of purpose. This frequently stems from the ability to see how one's role contributes to a bigger picture that everyone holds important. In fact, when this purpose is internalized, it can become a Personal Motivator.

By combining purpose with good leadership and strategy to realize a particular vision, organizational productivity increases and the picture becomes reality. However, the executive role does not end there; it always comes back to mission. From the very moment that the breath of life enters a company, it has a mission—a reason for existing. For us at Holden International, it has been and will always be to help sellers achieve personal and professional success. Most mission statements focus on value to others, and it is the responsibility of the executive team to communicate, protect, and advance this purpose for existing.

At the ground level, it is important to remember that although executives do not *generally* focus on daily management duties or operational activities, they are 100 percent responsible for them. The buck stops at the top. This means that executives need and strive for good visibility into their organizations, always on the alert to their reports "managing upward." This produces a nontraditional, yet informal, potential source of business value that is far up on the Sales Value Chain, providing discreet visibility into the company for executives. Although this is rarely discussed in any conference room, it's another arrow in the quiver of value for a Stage IV Customer Advisor.

Management Value

Managers compose the middle layer of an organization. Their job is to oversee operations in order to carry out the direction that the executive team sets. As such, they run specific functional areas of the business, such as Production, Engineering, or other departments. The point at which managers become executives varies by company. A head of a business unit or division that contains many functions might be viewed as an executive in one company and a senior manager in another.

The good news is that it doesn't really matter from your standpoint; you're positioning value for specific individuals, so you don't have to worry about what management category they fall within. Having said that, it is helpful to understand what is generally important to people as you move up the organization. Managers will often compare the return on investment (ROI) of your potential solution versus that of your competition or even against in-house alternatives. They may also notch the comparison up a level and look at competing projects.

When evaluating a supplier solution, managers tend to focus on business and operational value, along with total cost of ownership and cost/benefit, or ROI.

Operations Value

Forming the foundation of the organizational pyramid and making up the vast majority of an organization's employees are the *operators,* the individuals who actually do or support the work that generates revenue. For example, someone in procurement may purchase the components that go to manufacturing to be assembled by another operations person who works under the direction of a supervisor. We would consider all these individuals to be in operations. They carry out the organization's critical work, from working with customers to tweaking products to handling billing, all under the policies that management sets for them. It is their job to know the details.

During purchasing decisions, operators are often the ones who spend the most time evaluating the supplier at the nuts-and-bolts level. Do not underestimate their role or input; operators are often their company's product and system experts, and they are usually the people who are going to use whatever product they evaluate. A successful solution reflects positively on them, and at other times, an ineffective one will likely be a negative reflection on you.

Operators want to understand and test the features and functions of your proposed solution and often feel most comfortable with proven solutions, as they present lower risk for them to recommend.

Operators' managers typically want them to make a decision that produces a high-quality solution in the shortest time possible and at the lowest cost. They therefore need evidence from you that a solution will perform to their requirements and be a good fit for their department.

Positioning value in a relevant way starts with recognition of where an individual fits in the E-M-O Model. If you look at our completed E-M-O Model shown in Figure 9.2, you will see a two-sided arrow along the right side of the pyramid.

Figure 9.2
The E-M-O Model of Value Relevance

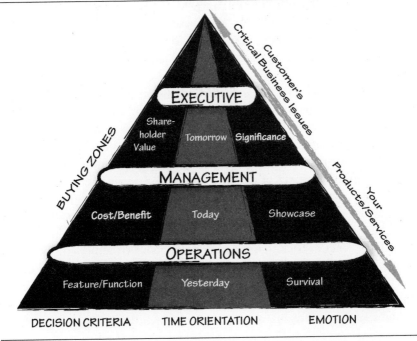

This emphasizes the point that the closer you are to the operators, the more freedom you have to talk about your products and services. In fact, operators will *want* to know the details. If, however, you are closer to the executives, you'll want to understand and focus on the company's vision, direction, and priorities, just as we discussed in terms of the Sales Value Chain.

Remember to check your products at the door whenever you meet with management or executives.

VALUE EXPRESSIONS

Armed with this E–M–O Model, Stage IV Customer Advisors use a process for packaging and articulating value that is based on customer collaboration up and down the Sales Value Chain. The result is to develop insight into the customer's business, politics, and culture in order to align your solution with the entire Sales Value Chain.

This manifests itself physically in the form of Value Statements and Value Propositions that are targeted to certain E–M–O customer levels and the business issues, initiatives, or priorities appropriate to those levels. So, as we just discussed in the prior section, the points you emphasize when meeting with operators differ greatly from those that would make sense when addressing an executive.

Value Statements refer to *qualitative* expressions of value, whereas Value Propositions are *quantitative* expressions of that same value. The former is more general and best suited to the early phases of a sales campaign when you don't have a lot of information but need to set up meetings with people to get that information. Value Statements project value to the customer and help highlight the benefit of meeting with you.

As a sales campaign progresses and you gain more insight into the customer's business, politics, and culture, the ultimate expression of value is when you identify the specific financial impact based on the right assumptions. This brings us back to our earlier point about customer collaboration: a Value Proposition is only as good as the assumptions on which it is based. It is therefore critical to discuss and develop these assumptions with a Situational Fox.

Think of it this way:

The credibility of your Value Proposition is only as good as is the level of influence of the customer who assisted you in formulating the assumptions behind it.

The more influential that person is, the more reliable your proposition will be.

Figure 9.3 summarizes the *what* and *why* of Value Statements and Value Propositions.

Figure 9.3
Value Expressions

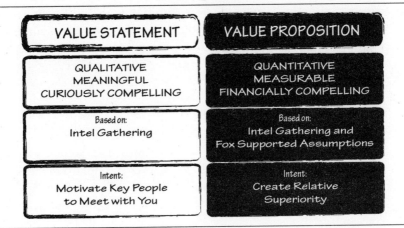

Now, let's look at the *how* for building Value Statements and Value Propositions, starting with the former. Keep in mind that multiple expressions of value will exist for a single solution and that a solution may change as you move up the Sales Value Chain.

VALUE STATEMENTS

Value Statements get you into the game, and to do that, they need to consist of four components:

1. *Critical Business Issues:* Goals, challenges, initiatives, or anything that is important at the E-M-O level on which you plan to focus your Value Statement. This is about *relevance.*
2. *Area of Improvement:* This includes the name of your solution, the part of the customer's organization that it will affect, and the operational nature of that impact. It is about *operational improvement.*
3. *Business Impact:* This part of the Value Statement translates operational improvement into business value. It is about *connecting* your solution's impact to the customer's critical business issues.
4. *Credibility:* Outlines your company's track record, references, experience, and/or expertise to ensure that you will be able to deliver the business impact identified. This is about *customer confidence.*

You need to focus on relevant customer business issues at the right organizational level with both solution clarity and supplier credibility.

Now, let's dive into a sample Value Statement. Assume that you are an account manager for a software company that specializes in retail solutions. Your target customer is a movie theater company with 100 locations and 1,000 screens that generates about $500 million in annual revenue. Your objective is to sell your company's new point-of-service (POS) software solution that would operate the movie theaters' food and beverage terminals. You will provide computerized cash registers that employees use when selling soda, candy, and popcorn.

- **Critical Business Issues:** Very quickly, you determine that your Value Statement must work at the customer executive level. You then launch into intel gathering in an attempt to discover the right *critical business issue.* The company's Chief Executive Officer (CEO) is getting ready for an initial public offering (IPO) of the company within the next two years, and both analyst reports and news coverage highlight that the key to a successful IPO is an increase in stand-alone movie theater profitability. You confirm via discussions with customer individuals that the CEO has announced a goal of increasing stand-alone movie theater profitability by at least 10 percent.
- **Area of Improvement:** This insight leads you to ask the question: How can your POS system help increase stand-alone movie theater profits by 10 percent? To answer this question, you need to discern potential *areas of improvement,* in terms of increasing revenue and lowering costs. Again, you accomplish this by gathering good intel—conducting customer research, making astute observations, and asking good questions. The result is twofold:
  - First, movie theaters make most of their profits from selling soda, candy, and popcorn. The ticket revenue essentially covers the cost of film distribution. Since you are not in a position to impact Hollywood economics, ticket pricing, or food/beverage promotions, you narrow in on how your POS solution can increase the number of customers each theater can serve at the concession stands. It all comes down to throughput.
  - Second, your solution will have a lower total cost of ownership (TCO) than your competitor's, but their price is slightly lower. However, their system is expensive to maintain and does not integrate with other systems as easily as yours does. It therefore requires more time and money to support.
- **Business Impact:** Next, you estimate that the *business impact* of more customers served and a lower TCO will result in higher revenue and lower costs.

- **Credibility:** Finally, you think about what *credibility* you will project. You point to similar successful installations for which your company is responsible within the industry.

Add all this up, and you get the executive-focused Value Statement in Figure 9.4.

Figure 9.4
Value Statement Template and Example

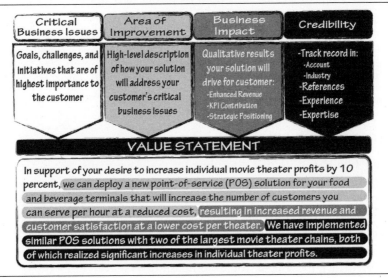

TESTING VALUE STATEMENTS

It is helpful to first test a Value Statement's integrity before going live with the customer. To accomplish this, we ask three questions:

1. Is the Value Statement relevant to the target audience?
2. Is the solution aligned with the right critical business issue?
3. Is the value provided distinctive from that of the competition?

Applying this test to our theater example yields the following results:

- Is the Value Statement relevant to the target audience? Yes, it is targeted to the CEO and addresses the IPO.
- Have you aligned your solution with the right critical business issue? Yes, the POS solution will increase individual movie theater profits, which is crucial to the success of the IPO. You also demonstrated a clear understanding of the business by the way you explained the solution, which is equally important.

- Do you provide value that is distinctive from that of the competition? Yes, for two reasons. First, your solution carries a lower TCO than that of the competition. Second, and perhaps more important, you established yourself as a Stage IV Customer Advisor in the customer's eyes by showing thought leadership. This is a nontraditional source of relative superiority.

Remember that in most cases, a Value Statement is designed to help you gain access to key people and find your way into the Situational Power Base. Don't be surprised if you find that you need to modify your solution, target a different critical business issue, or even refocus to a different person or customer level *during* such a meeting. It's common to move up and down the Sales Value Chain during a sales campaign. The point is that you are outselling your competition by providing customer value that produces nontraditional sources of relative superiority.

THE VALUE PROPOSITION

Quantifying the value that you identify in a Value Statement is a powerful source of customer impact and supplier credibility. Value Propositions summarize your business case and show how your solution is economically compelling for the customer. They may also be operationally focused and quantify operational impact, if your focus is on the operations level of the customer organization.

In particular, it outlines:

- The nature and extent of business or operational impact and improvement.
- When that impact will be realized.
- The metrics that will enable you and your customer to monitor and manage progress.

A Value Proposition's math does not have to be perfect; rather, you want to *build it collaboratively with a customer individual who is in the Power Base*— preferably a Fox. We cannot emphasize this enough; it is critical for two reasons:

1. The insight you receive from someone in the know will significantly sharpen your case, because it will be more accurate, complete, and current.
2. A Value Proposition is only as good as the assumptions on which it is based. These assumptions must be arrived at through collaboration with a Power Base member or directly with a Fox. It is only then that the assumptions will carry the credibility of the Fox within the customer organization.

In most cases, you will not arrive at a completed Value Proposition in just one or two meetings. It is typically the result of collaboration with the right people over time. If you are working with a Situational Fox, the time frame will likely be short. *If you focus on individuals who are outside of the Power Base, however, it could take much, much longer.*

We use a three-step Value Proposition Road Map, shown in Figure 9.5, to guide this collaboration and development.

Figure 9.5
Building a Value Proposition

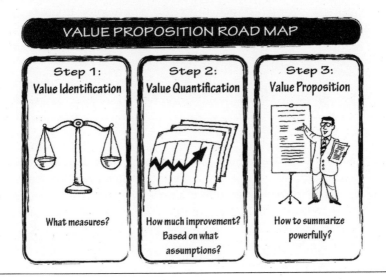

VALUE PROPOSITION ROAD MAP

| Step 1: Value Identification | Step 2: Value Quantification | Step 3: Value Proposition |
| What measures? | How much improvement? Based on what assumptions? | How to summarize powerfully? |

Step 1: Value Identification

This step is straightforward; it's based on your Value Statement and the connection between your solution and creating business or operational impact. The real challenge is constructing the value metrics with which you'll measure that impact. Generally speaking, these metrics will focus on effectiveness and efficiency measures that track and quantify activities or results that will contribute directly or indirectly to business or operational value. They need to be specific in nature. For example, a suitable metric in our theater scenario might be concession stand sales per hour.

Step 2: Value Quantification

Once you have identified the value metrics on which to focus, your next step is to project the total impact or value to the customer. To do this, we utilize the simple value quantification worksheet shown in Figure 9.6.

Figure 9.6
Value Quantification, Step 2 in Value Proposition
Road Map—Theater Example

Step 2: VALUE QUANTIFICATION

METRIC	- A - What is it Now? (# or %)	- B - What is the Goal? (# or %)	- C - What is the Difference? (B − A = C)	- D - Value of One "A"? ($)	- E - Value of the Difference? (C x D = E)
#Customers served per hour per theater	100 customers	120 customers	20 customers	$3.2m across all theaters	$64m
Total cost of ownership for POS system	$5m	$4m	20%		$1m

A good guideline is to focus on the most important value metrics—the ones you identified in collaboration with a member of the customer's Power Base. The example shown in Figure 9.6 displays one metric on revenue increase (the number of customers served per hour per theater) as well as one on cost reduction (total cost of ownership for the POS system). Assume that the Situational Fox takes you to the Finance Department to confirm that their current average is about 100 customers served per hour per theater, as shown in column A.

Column B indicates the goal, or what your solution makes possible. Based on the faster speed of your system or higher throughput—and due mainly to ease of use—you and the Fox make the assumption that an increase of about 20 customers is reasonable. Column C shows a difference of 20 customers per hour. In column D, you jointly make another assumption about the value of one customer per hour across all hours of operation and all theaters, which equates to about $3.2 million.

There are certainly additional assumptions that you and the Fox needed to make about the average price per customer and customer traffic per theater per hour. To figure this out, you asked the Fox whether someone in finance or operations could help provide the right information; in each case, the Fox helped set up meetings and conference calls.

Finally, you and the Fox estimate that if a faster POS system is able to increase customers served per hour by 20 percent, then the annual value of that difference across all theaters would be about $64 million (shown in column E). You don't spend too much time worrying whether it is $60 million or $70 million; you are going for directional magnitude validated by the customer.

You repeat the same process for total cost of ownership for the POS system and conclude with the Fox that your solution's TCO will be about $1 million less than the customer's current solution. This recognition of value prompts the Fox to introduce you to more people in the IT Department, perhaps in order to validate the details of switching costs for the new system.

Step 3: Value Proposition

Now you are ready to create the Value Proposition that identifies how much value you'll provide, when the customer will realize it, and how you can measure it. Figure 9.7 summarizes this.

Figure 9.7
Value Proposition, Step 3 in Value Proposition
Road Map—Theater Example

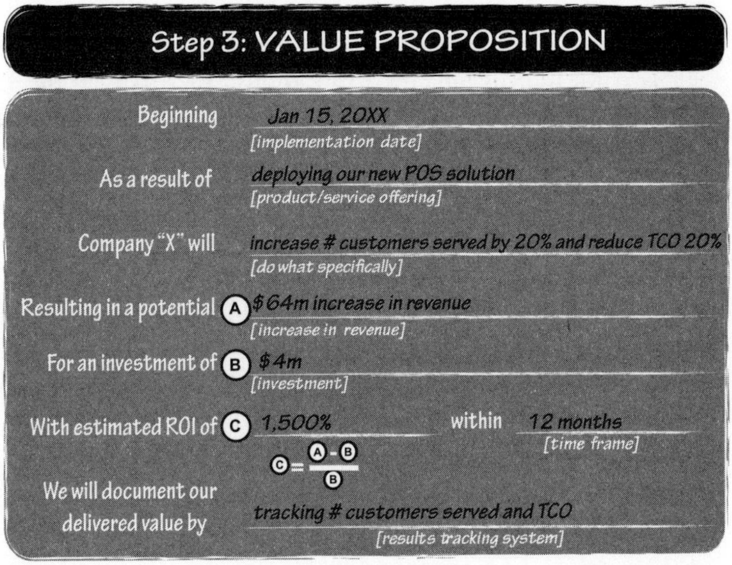

Step 3: VALUE PROPOSITION

Beginning	Jan 15, 20XX [implementation date]
As a result of	deploying our new POS solution [product/service offering]
Company "X" will	increase # customers served by 20% and reduce TCO 20% [do what specifically]
Resulting in a potential (A)	$64m increase in revenue [increase in revenue]
For an investment of (B)	$4m [investment]
With estimated ROI of (C)	1,500% within 12 months [time frame] $C = \dfrac{A - B}{B}$
We will document our delivered value by	tracking # customers served and TCO [results tracking system]

What is a more powerful claim: that your POS system is faster and cheaper? Or, being able to credibly tell the customer that "It will create about $64 million of new revenue, while decreasing costs by $1 million, all within the next year before your IPO"?

Remember the Power Base Principle:

VALUE + RECOGNITION = POWER

If your value is differentiated, but not recognized by the customer Power Base, it will prove to be a meaningless math exercise.

To see how this plays out, imagine three different scenarios.

Scenario #1: You present your Value Proposition to the Fox, who asks, "Where did you get those numbers?" To which you respond, "They are based on industry best practices." Now the Fox must invest time and energy validating the sources. The meeting comes to a standstill while she continues asking questions in an attempt to confirm your data. She will probably not be able to commit to a next step in the buying process until she further investigates the numbers.

Scenario #2: In the same situation you respond, "I worked with Joe Stanford." To which the Fox asks, "Who is Joe Stanford?" As it turns out, Joe is not in the Power Base. Therefore, the Fox does not trust the numbers, putting you in a worse position than in scenario #1.

Scenario #3: The same situation again, but now you respond, "I worked with Jana Meader in Finance." You know that Jana is in the Power Base and that the Fox knows her. The Fox may well validate what you have said but will also tend to turn her focus to implementation issues. At this point, you have shortened the sales cycle and increased your potential to create relative superiority and win the business.

Lastly, keep in mind that Value Statements and Value Propositions may change as you move up the E-M-O continuum, or you may develop one expression of value that applies to all levels of the customer organization.

MOVING UP THE SALES VALUE CHAIN TO INCLUDE POLITICAL VALUE

Assume that the Chief Information Officer (CIO) in our theater example is the Situational Fox. His Personal Motivator is to enhance the perception among the senior executives, particularly the CEO, that the IT Department is more than a cost center; it can be a strategic business asset that drives new revenue. Because your POS solution supports this Personal Motivator, we will assume that the CIO is a Supporter. Do you have an opportunity to convert him to an Ally? This brings us back to the difference between expected value and Unexpected Value. The POS solution will provide solid but expected value, while the key to forming Allies often relies on your ability to offer Unexpected Value.

This is where a Stage IV Customer Advisor shines. As a member of a major software company, you realize that your company trains thousands of software developers each year. They use hotels and conference centers to conduct the training; however, you find out that your Technical Training Department does not care what type of venue you use as long as it fits within their budget. You then discover that your customer's movie theaters sit vacant before noon every day of the year.

By combining that intel with your unconventional thinking, you approach the customer's CIO with an idea as to how the two of you could convince your company to use the movie theaters each morning for the software training. Intrigued, the customer CIO agrees to collaborate with you to build a Value Proposition. The two of you estimate that such an approach could bring in roughly $10 million of additional revenue for the movie theater company, while also reducing your company's cost of training by 15 percent.

The approach here is to demonstrate that the customer's IT group can function as a nontraditional source of business advantage and that the POS solution example is not an anomaly or one-time event in terms of your demonstrating thought leadership. When executive management sees the POS solution and the software training incremental revenue initiative together, it further establishes the customer's IT group as a strategic asset and you as a Customer Advisor. Moreover, who gets the credit—and whose Personal Motivator is advanced? The customer CIO gains the recognition and a seat at the table with the executives, while you now are more aligned with the Enterprise Power Base by having moved up the Sales Value Chain.

You can see how this increases your ability to win business and advance the penetration and development of accounts. The next chapter shows you a process to reach the pinnacle of Value Creation by creating new demand with customer executives to displace competitors and grow important accounts.

CHAPTER 10

CREATING DEMAND TO DISPLACE COMPETITORS

A wise man will make more opportunities than he finds.

—Francis Bacon

The hallmark of a Stage IV Customer Advisor is *not* to just do what every other seller on the planet does—service demand. Not to discount the significance of defeating competitors while servicing demand, as it is clearly no easy task. However, Stage IV focuses on the pinnacle of sales effectiveness—the rarefied air where individuals apply unconventional thinking to the task of creating demand and actually become catalysts who generate sales opportunities. They understand very well that 95 percent of the time, the seller who forms the business wins the business.

Customer Advisors also realize that there is no more powerful approach to penetrating a competitively held account than to formulate a strategy that is based on creating demand. This attaches an extended significance to the above 95 percent rule, thereby enabling the seller to win the battle and grow in strength—in other words, create a new opportunity and leverage the resulting win to drive a wedge into the account and displace the competition.

Unlike servicing demand—where sellers can sometimes get away with counting on what they are selling versus how they are selling in order to win—creating demand works only in the "how" domain. It is all about *you,* the seller—not the product or service. Specifically, it requires you to discover the potential to create Unexpected Value along with a plan that enables the customer to realize that value, thereby creating market share that does not exist. This is where the simple process of sales transitions into *business development.* See Figure 10.1.

Figure 10.1
The Pinnacle of Value Creation

In the next section, we cover the significance in the distinction between creating and servicing demand. We then introduce a process that leverages creating demand to penetrate competitively held accounts, which will put you at the epicenter of Stage IV Customer Advisor account management.

CREATING DEMAND SIGNIFICANCE

Creating demand is attractive to customers because it represents the essence of customer value: accelerating their business in a way they did not anticipate, as we have discussed earlier. It disproportionately accelerates quota achievement for sellers because it is often single-sourced business. Therefore, if it goes to bid, the request for proposal (RFP) is essentially wired to support the supplier who has created the opportunity, which results in:

- High win rates that can be forecasted early and accurately but that may lead to . . .
- . . . a longer-than-usual sales cycle the first time around with a customer. The second time you create demand with a specific customer you will likely see a relatively short sales cycle. All of this adds up to . . .
- . . . high-margin business, as the customer's willingness to pay for Unexpected Value is maximized.

Now, let's contrast this to servicing demand. In that scenario, a seller wins a deal because demand exists for his or her solution; sometimes it is already present, and sometimes sellers create it. Occasionally, it's a combination of both. So, what contributes to this demand? Sometimes it's circumstantial, such as selling in a booming industry or when you're representing a category killer product that everybody wants. You may be aligned with a Fox when servicing these identified deals and not even know it. You've likely witnessed a sales situation in which a powerful person provides you with direction and guidance. Foxes are known to seek out sellers who can assist them, even if the seller is not exactly aware of what is happening. All these circumstances are welcome; they produce a low-intensity selling environment that provides a nice break from the more typical high-intensity competitive sales campaigns that tend to represent today's selling world. Lastly, servicing demand often takes place at the operations level of the customer organization, as the business value has already been established. This is in contrast to creating demand, which occurs at multiple levels of the Sales Value Chain.

If we can't find the opportunities that we need to achieve quota, we need to make them. In creating demand, *you* create the opportunity. For starters, you have to be aligned with a Fox. By definition, there is no budget. You need someone powerful enough to create the budget or pull it from someplace (and someone) else. You will also need a Fox to lead the charge, as some people will likely resist new thinking and ideas that they might consider disruptive.

Only a Fox has the power, network, and diplomatic skills to grapple with opposition without offending or alienating key people. At the worst, people may view a Fox as unreasonable; at the best, they're simply unseen. Stage IV Customer Advisors have a lot in common with Foxes in this regard. The following quote from George Bernard Shaw summarizes this situation, "The reasonable man adapts to the world: the unreasonable one persists in trying to adapt the world to himself. Therefore, all progress depends on the unreasonable man." Creating your own opportunities is adapting the world to you. Selling at this level puts you in the ranks of the unreasonable.

Our deal experience shows that there are two opportune times for creating demand. The first occurs when a Fox who moves into a new position with a different company drafts you. If you have provided solutions that map into the Sales Value Chain in the past, leveraged the Power Base Principle, and advanced the Fox's Personal Motivator, chances are that he or she will want you to become an extended part of his or her Power Base. The Fox's intent is to replicate the success of the past. The Fox must also establish himself or herself quickly in this new position, which helps you, as it tends to shorten sales cycle times.

As such, the Fox will call you to collaborate on *new* types of value that you could provide, because simply introducing a "different flavor" of an existing solution that is in place produces no real recognition. Instead, the Fox needs Unexpected Value to make a highly recognized contribution to his or her new company. Remember:

VALUE + RECOGNITION = POWER

That is why creating demand lends itself so well to this drafting phenomenon.

The second opportune time takes place when you need to penetrate a competitively held account. This is when the process that we are about to introduce will become your friend; all sellers know how difficult it is to gain a foothold when on competitive terrain. But the value of doing so is profoundly significant to your company. In addition, if you can create demand to spark a process that penetrates a competitively held account, it will be fairly simple to expand business in an existing account.

LEVERAGING CREATING DEMAND TO PENETRATE ACCOUNTS

Figure 10.2 introduces a process that is as logical as it is stealthy. Its unconventional nature will translate to counterintuitiveness for many of your competitors, giving you the cover of darkness. Only during the later stages of the process will some competitors begin to see what you are doing; still, many will dismiss it, because they don't understand it. These are the sellers who blame a fluke situation that will not repeat itself when they lose.

It's usually not a problem if your competitor is at Stage I or II. However, a Stage III Compete Seller may detect what you're up to around Step 5. And, if you find yourself up against a Stage IV Customer Advisor, he or she might have a clue at Step 4 or possibly earlier. Having said that, our data show that 80 percent of all sellers are at Stages I and II; therefore, most of them will not understand what you are doing even after you have done it. To protect yourself against the more advanced Stage III and IV sellers, you must move quickly and quietly through the process. Remember that time is *not* on your side. The steps to follow in the entry penetration process are shown in Figure 10.2 and explained further in the following section.

Figure 10.2
Account Penetration Process

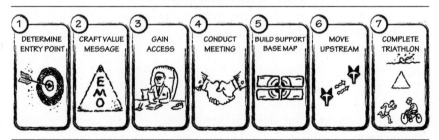

| 1 DETERMINE ENTRY POINT | 2 CRAFT VALUE MESSAGE | 3 GAIN ACCESS | 4 CONDUCT MEETING | 5 BUILD SUPPORT BASE MAP | 6 MOVE UPSTREAM | 7 COMPLETE TRIATHLON |

STEP 1: DETERMINE THE ENTRY POINT

You begin your account penetration that leverages creating demand by identifying the right point of entry, that is, which business unit or functional area you should focus on within an account. It's about knowing what doors to knock on as your initial penetration point. To sort this out, you take four factors into consideration:

1. Political connectivity
2. Business significance
3. Business impact
4. Supplier return

These factors work in concert to help you quickly and objectively determine where to start the process of displacing a competitor from a potentially important account. Let's look at each one in detail.

1. *Political Connectivity:* Is there a Fox in a particular business unit, division, or department who has a relationship with a higher-level Fox? This is important because when you determine how to provide a specific business unit with Unexpected Value by moving up the Sales Value Chain, you will want to move upstream to the higher-level Fox with the support of the Situational Fox with whom you are working. This is why it's critical to engage in intel gathering to discover this kind of Fox-to-Fox connectivity.

2. *Business Significance:* Which business unit or functional area is the most financially or strategically crucial to the company? Although the obvious choice is one that produces the most revenue or profit, sometimes it is one that has the potential to directly or indirectly drive revenue and/or margin in the future. In that case, it would be considered strategic. As with the first factor, you want to lean heavily on your intel gathering to make as accurate an assessment as possible. This becomes significant because the upstreaming that we mentioned earlier may not work if you focus on an ancillary—and therefore, not very important—part of the customer's business.

3. *Business Impact:* In which business unit or functional area can the solution you provide make a significant impact? This is probably the most challenging factor to assess because you may not have sufficient information to determine how you will move up the Sales Value Chain within any specific functional area. To address this, consider the intel you have gathered and be ready to apply it to multiple

business units, divisions, or departments if necessary. There is simply no easy way to avoid doing your homework on this one. Determining business impact becomes an important step even if you are working with a significant business unit, as making an insignificant contribution will likely prevent you from moving upstream later.

4. *Supplier Return:* Which business unit or functional area will provide your company with an acceptable return? Keep in mind that some of the account penetration cost can be amortized over the business generated during the next few years if your penetration effort is successful. At the same time, you certainly want your first deal to be profitable; that is why it is so important to move up the Sales Value Chain to protect margins. In addition, providing Unexpected Value will also play a key role in your ability to upstream to the higher-level Fox.

Now, let's look at each of these steps through the lens of an example. Suppose that there is a major bank in your territory that you have not been able to penetrate. Your immediate task objective is to determine the right entry point, so you begin by launching your intel-gathering effort. It becomes clear before long that one of three business units could be your target: wholesale banking, community banking, or wealth management.

Political Connectivity

You then focus on the first entry point factor, political connectivity. Heading up each of the business units is a Senior Vice President (SVP) who reports to the bank's Chief Executive Officer (CEO). As it turns out, the SVP of Wholesale is not in the Enterprise Power Base. Although he's very senior and well respected, he is also close to retirement. The head of community banking, however, is powerful and definitely part of the Enterprise Power Base, whose Fox is the CEO. The problem there is that you have found out that he is an Opponent when it comes to your company—bad news, indeed! At the same time, your intel suggests that the SVP of Wealth Management may be accessible, but her political strength is questionable. *Although it is not what you would like it to be, the best Fox-to-Fox connectivity seems to reside within community banking.*

Business Significance

Fortunately, the second factor in determining where to focus—business significance—is more straightforward. Wholesale banking, which centers on other banks and large corporations, is down in both revenue and margin, whereas wealth management has done well, largely due to its transaction fee business model. But the growth play is clearly in community banking, particularly from a margin point of view. *As such, you decide that the business significance thumbs up needs to go to community banking.*

Business Impact

Business impact will always be business unit specific, so you are now ready to make an assessment of impact potential. Appropriately, your intel gathering focuses on community banking in order to build a much deeper understanding of that business.

After conducting the detailed research, making a few calls, and exercising one or two social network connections, you're getting a clearer picture of how to provide Unexpected Value. Customer checks are processed manually at the branch level. You know from experience that if the bank were to employ check imaging technology, they could potentially reduce labor by probably one full-time employee (FTE) per branch. After doing the math for the total number of branches, it appears that your solution could save the bank the equivalent of their entire telecommunications budget—and that doesn't even take into account the positive effect on customer satisfaction and retention. Equally exciting is the option of freeing up customer service personnel to focus on selling new services to existing clients, as this is becoming a priority in the community banking unit. But perhaps best of all is the fact that the bank has no idea that all this is possible, which means that this is your opportunity to move well up the Sales Value Chain to provide Unexpected Value. *Although the cost savings or refocusing of personnel would not be a home run, it would certainly get you to second base—another vote for community banking as your entry point.*

Supplier Return

The last step is to address supplier return. You have experience with this type of solution and know that little to no discounting is required for the deal to be profitable. Certainly, you'll have to provide a proof of concept exercise during which you will set up a test installation within a few branches to demonstrate the approach and assess the business impact. But if history repeats itself, that should go well. *As such, another check mark goes next to community banking to be your target.*

STEP 2: CRAFT YOUR VALUE MESSAGE

Now you apply what you learned in Chapter 8 to form an executive Value Statement. If you have time and enough information, take a first pass at a

Value Proposition in which you quantify the value that you believe you can provide. Remember, however, that you will need help from a Fox or someone in the Power Base to form the assumptions upon which your Value Proposition is based.

STEP 3: GAIN ACCESS

The initial purpose of a draft Value Statement is to help you gain access to the Power Base by providing the right person with a reason to meet with you. You will recall from our earlier example that the Fox of community banking is an Opponent. So what is the best way to handle this?

Many would advise you to go to someone else. That might make sense if the person you approach is in the Power Base—specifically, an Emerging Fox. But generally speaking, we think otherwise. Instead, we suggest that you go directly to your Opponent, using your Value Statement. If that doesn't work, and it may well not, get to an Emerging Fox or anyone in the Fox's Power Base.

Your task is to get a meeting. This isn't going to be easy, considering that the Fox is an Opponent. However, these kinds of meetings can be as rewarding for some sellers as they are intimidating for others. If you are able to meet with the Fox, the likelihood of changing his mind is actually quite high. You must be professional but tenacious. Since your Opponent will probably be reluctant to meet with you, let's look at a few tips that might help you gain access to the executive. Figure 10.3 illustrates this.

Figure 10.3
Ways to Get a Meeting with an Executive

- **If you've already met, then engage!** This may sound obvious; however, our deal experience shows that too many sellers hesitate to just pick up the phone and call an executive whom they have already met. Keeping our example in mind, this is particularly helpful if you know someone who knows your Opponent. Depending on the size of the organization, you may need to build rapport with an executive assistant to ensure he or she shares your value message with the Fox. Depending on what you learn about the Fox's style, you may choose to send an email or handwritten note, and then follow up with a call.

- **Get sponsored by the Power Base.** If you do not have a relationship with the executive, particularly an Opponent, the best scenario is to leverage the strength of the person's own Power Base. You are much more likely to get first meeting if you are referred from within the Fox's Power Base. You will still need a draft Value Statement, but in this case, your contact in the account will communicate the value message that will help you get the meeting.

- **Look for shared connections in social media.** Review your social media connections and see if you have any in common. Is there anyone in your personal network, such as a former classmate or colleague, who may help you gain access?

- **Leverage your company's executives.** Is there someone from your own organization or board of directors who could help?

- **Network with your suppliers and alliance partners.** Does your company have a supplier or an alliance partner that could make an introduction? Perhaps this is an opportunity for a seller to increase the value he or she can bring to your company by helping you.

- **Arrange a meeting at an industry, social, or charitable event.** Is there an upcoming professional, charitable, or social event where you could make contact with a key person? Keep in mind that many companies sponsor such events.

- **Cold call.** If all other methods do not grant you access, then polish up your Value Statement, pick up the phone, and call!

STEP 4: CONDUCT A MEETING

In general, you should set four objectives when preparing for an executive meeting in order to move up the Sales Value Chain and determine how to provide Unexpected Value. If you are dealing with an Opponent, fold the advice provided in Chapter 7 into the preparation and execution of the meeting.

1. *Establish your credibility* early in the meeting by using your intel.
2. *Demonstrate that you are able to contribute as a thought leader,* suggesting unconventional possibilities to advancing the customer's business.
3. *Initiate a relationship;* talk about what you and your company believe in to establish a cultural fit, if it exists. If it does not, look for common personal ground where you may have overlapping interests.
4. *Gain the executive's explicit sponsorship* and support to work together to further develop your draft Value Statement and then form the right set of assumptions that will lead to a sound Value Proposition.

There is no "one best way" to run an executive meeting; much of it hinges on the type of access you achieve and your ability to react in real time to what the executive says to you. For example, if you are able to secure a five-minute meeting at an industry conference, you need to get to your point quickly. Conversely, if you are able to arrange a one-hour briefing, you will be able to proceed in more detail. Keep in mind that some of the best encounters can be brief and unplanned!

You need to demonstrate your interpersonal skills, diplomacy, and intellect during all customer interactions. When meetings with customer executives go well, they go very well—but when they don't, you have a serious problem in the account. And this doesn't apply only to you. You're in the same amount of trouble if you include a manager who makes an off-color remark, inappropriately challenges the executive, or makes unrealistic commitments.

In addition, it's vital to match the pace of the executive. If he or she is slow and methodical, choosing words carefully and listening to what you say with the intent of observing you, then you must do the same. Remember that observing is applying judgment or inference to what is being said. You must observe and not just listen. Going back to our point on pace, if the executive speaks quickly with a more rapid cadence, then be sure to keep up. Avoid lengthy explanations, and stick to the relevant essence of your responses. This accomplishes two things: First, it communicates that you know what you are talking about because you can net it out. Second, it strikes compatibility with the executive in matching how he or she likes to communicate.

Engaging with Advanced Communicators

The higher up you go in an organization, the more you should be prepared to engage in advanced communication methods. Two styles you may encounter include:

- *Metaphorical.* Some advanced communicators may use metaphors to either help people understand what they are saying or to transmit information to select people in the room who they know will understand the metaphor. They control who will understand the message by selecting the analog environment. For example, if the person to whom they want to transmit a particular point has an understanding of farming and no one else in the room has this understanding, then a farming metaphor will do the job nicely. The same could be said for sports metaphors or any other subject.

  In addition, unlike other forms of communication, metaphors evoke emotion to make an impression. For example, saying that "a seller is drowning in orders" projects a stronger positive impression than saying "the seller has a good backlog." Advanced communicators use this tool for persuasion and motivation purposes, as well as to selectively enhance understanding.
- *Purely Conceptual.* On rare occasions, some advanced communicators find it easier to sort out a difficult problem or situation in the *abstract* and then translate the answer or approach into an operational expression that all can understand. For example, if you say that the presentation contained a *kaleidoscopic* textual quality, you could mean several things, one of which might be that the presentation was very appealing, like the colors of a kaleidoscope, or that it was complete, as reflected in the full color spectrum. You could also mean that it was substantial, in terms of the endless depth of a kaleidoscope. As you can see, this example has a metaphorical element, which suggests that an understanding of both the metaphor and the general context within which the executive is speaking is helpful.

Whether this is new to you or not, when meeting with senior executives, we recommend that you always:

- **Take good notes.** Capture all that you can. Although this is always a good idea, it is essential when you are dealing with an advanced communicator. You can take time later to think through what he or she said, including the nuances. Then you can express your understanding as part of a follow-up email, which is perfectly acceptable.
- **Ask questions.** The executive may test you by speaking in a manner that he or she knows you will not likely understand. Even if you *do* understand, asking a question that takes the discussion into more depth—as long as it is relevant to the executive's point—will demonstrate and enhance your understanding.

Executive Meeting Checklist

In an ideal world, an executive meeting might go something like that shown in Figure 10.4. But even if all does not go according to plan, it is still important to have a process and know what you want to accomplish. After all, as the famous chemist Louis Pasteur wisely said, "Change favors the prepared mind."

Figure 10.4
Executive Meeting Checklist

SPONSORSHIP TO BUILD VALUE PROPOSITION

1. **Capture attention.** Establish credibility and rapport by sharing insight regarding the customer's business, industry, company, or customers. Senior executives are motivated to meet with external thought leaders to gain objective market insight, which they cannot always get from the people who report to them. Earn the right to talk about *your* company as it relates to the customer's business. For example, if you are speaking with a Chief Information Officer (CIO), share emerging trends in information technology (IT) that could enable him to significantly advance his company's growth objectives.
2. **Engage critical business issue.** Confirm your understanding of the issues most critical to the customer's business success. Focus on observation, asking questions that drive deeper understanding and insight, while connecting that insight to what your company can provide whenever it makes sense. Keep your place on the Sales Value

Chain in mind, and work to move north based on your customer knowledge and solution flexibility. It is powerful when you can formulate a solution or even the basis for a solution in real time during one of these executive meetings.

3. **Test your Value Statement.** Having formed a solution or, again, even a framework for a solution, experiment with your questions to determine how to most clearly articulate your Value Statement. Make certain that there is a direct or indirect connection to the customer priorities, moving as high up as possible on the Sales Value Chain.

4. **Share your draft Value Proposition.** If you are comfortable with your Value Statement and have a draft of your Value Proposition, present it in an exploratory way to him. As you know, translating your Value Statement to a Value Proposition requires that you make the right assumptions with the right people. Do this well and your value messaging will carry significant credibility and create high customer impact. Having said that, the executive with whom you are speaking may not be able to help you with those assumptions. This won't be a problem as long as he or she sponsors you to the person who *can* assist you: an individual in the Power Base.

5. **Secure sponsorship.** The executive response to your request for sponsorship will be only as good as the relevance and credibility of your Value Statement and how close you are to advancing the executive's Personal Motivator. As such, it is useful to spend some time during the meeting working to understand what is important to the executive. It's best for this to occur informally whenever possible, perhaps during a break.

6. **Confirm a return ticket.** Before you conclude the meeting, agree on how you will report back to the executive. Suggest that you will close the loop with her only at significant points in the process. You don't need to send the executive an email informing her that you've set a meeting with someone she recommended. Instead, report back after you have met with the other person on the magnitude of the financial impact your solution could have on their business. That is a noteworthy matter that warrants touching base with the executive.

STEP 5: BUILD YOUR SUPPORT BASE MAP

Again, the engine to penetrating a competitively held account is creating demand, which can be summarized as the process of moving up the Sales Value Chain in order to provide the customer with Unexpected Value. Later in this chapter, we discuss how to leverage that value from an account penetration point of view. But for now, let's look at the critical mass of support within the customer organization required to create demand. Specifically, what support is required and by whom?

There is no absolute rule here, as individuals may perform multiple functions; however, there are several maxims that we have learned from extensive deal reviews. In particular, you want to look for the following:

- **An Executive Sponsor:** This may be a Fox or Emerging Fox within a business unit, division, or department. As we mentioned earlier in the book, Fox involvement in creating demand is a must, because the effort will not get off the ground without the ability to see the potential to create value and the internal power to push the idea into a proof of concept phase. As such, the Fox provides both insight and influence.

- **A Financial Supporter:** This individual is often a part of the finance group within the business unit or at corporate. This person is necessary because in the absence of funding, you will need him or her to perform some financial reprioritizing and sourcing to fund the unexpected solution.

- **An Operational Sponsor:** This person will shepherd the proof of concept exercise and oversee and manage the new solution's implementation. Why is this significant? Because it is human nature for some people to oppose new and innovative thinking. When opposition takes place at the operations level, constant oversight is necessary to keep the project on track.

- **End User Supporters:** These are people who will use the new solution on a day-to-day basis. The "why" for these folks is straightforward. They are another source of insight that may guide you in developing the solution and can be helpful in supporting a proof of concept exercise. As a group, they can become a significant source of support or resistance. Although often overlooked, they are key players.

Sponsors can be thought of as active drivers of a new initiative, while supporters enable a new initiative. Both are important.

STEP 6: MOVE UPSTREAM

As soon as you have achieved results during the proof of concept exercise, it is time to upstream. This requires that you revisit the Fox-to-Fox relationship that we discussed earlier, as you will be asking the Business Unit Fox to sponsor a meeting with the Enterprise Fox at corporate. That meeting will give you the chance to present the goals, approach, and results of the proof of concept exercise, along with the implications to the customer's business if it is rolled out. Two factors help to ensure that this meeting takes place:

1. You tap into the power of the Business Unit Fox and depend on his or her relationship with the Enterprise Fox. You know that this exists, because the Business Unit Fox is in the Power Base of the Enterprise Fox.
2. You provide Unexpected Value, which is always more exciting and impactful than expected value.

This gives you the opportunity to begin building a relationship with, let's say, the company's CEO. This might not be possible unless you are a CEO yourself—or an industry guru—which is why sellers tend to bring in senior management to get meetings with high-level customer executives. Although that makes sense, it underscores the account development power of creating demand. *More specifically, it gives you more access to corporate executives who can provide you with more insight to uncover the opportunity to create more demand. It produces a feedback loop that will continue to operate as long as you continue to bring value.*

STEP 7: COMPLETE THE TRIATHLON

So far, we have discussed the process of creating demand and upstreaming to the corporate executive level within a customer's organization. The third and final element to completing the triathlon is to expand your footprint in the account by servicing demand. The point here is to create a critical mass of installed base in order to secure the account. Creating demand makes you highly competitive in this regard. You now have a Support Base that will drive up your win potential in a way that did not exist before you launched your creating demand initiative.

But make no mistake, as you build your installed base, people *will* expect more of you. The customer will want you to comply with all the requirements of a bid but will also want to see some innovative thinking. You'll probably work with new people within the account who know exactly what Unexpected Value can do for one's career. They will want you to add a layer of creating demand on top of your more traditional solutions. It does not need to be revolutionary, but it does need to keep you higher up on the Sales Value Chain. This type of out-of-the-box thinking may relate to the products or services that you provide; it might involve other customers, your executive team, or your R&D group. But however you accomplish it, you absolutely must do so to fully leverage a creating demand initiative and further the penetration and development of an account.

PENETRATING COMPETITIVELY HELD ACCOUNTS

Now let's examine how you might apply this process to a competitively held account. Going back to our banking example from earlier in the chapter, assume that the competition is working in all three business units that we identified. In fact, the SVPs of wholesale banking, community banking, and wealth management are potentially all aligned with the competition, who has an installed base in each business unit. So, how do you penetrate the account?

You'll probably have a difficult time getting a meeting with an SVP, so where do you start? You can launch your effort by gathering intel and progressing along the seven steps that we outlined earlier—but in a much more indirect manner. You still need to identify which business unit to focus on; we'll assume it's community banking. And as before, this will require that you make midlevel contacts to gain intel and some degree of support. But you also need to produce inroads into IT and Finance. In a quick but quiet way, you get to someone in the Power Base of IT, ideally an Emerging Fox who may not be covered by the competition. You then connect your community banking contact with your IT contact to develop the concept of a technology-enabled solution that will reduce or redirect labor content through check imaging.

As you progress to the point of producing a draft Value Proposition, you make contact with a member of the Finance Department or perhaps Marketing if your focus is going to be on the value of upselling existing clients. He will review and improve the assumptions on which the Value Proposition is based. Unlike the other business units, however, you go for the Fox within Finance or Marketing.

Penetrating a competitively held account is all about quietly establishing a proof of concept. We refer to this as your Prime Objective—a critical task objective that, if accomplished, indicates high win potential.

Certainly, the SVP of Community Banking will become aware of what you are doing and will need to approve it, but you don't need that to happen in a vacuum. You just need to make enough progress in order to secure a meeting with him or her. At the end of the day, creating demand doesn't do your selling for you; it opens doors that lead to opportunity within accounts. It will be up to you, having gained access (Step 3), conducted the meeting (Step 4), and improved your Support Base (Step 5), to obtain a green light for the proof of concept exercise, thus achieving your Prime Objective.

With a successful proof of concept, everything else proceeds as we presented earlier. You upstream with the endorsement of the SVP of Community Banking to the CEO and begin to build relationships at the corporate executive level. This in turn significantly strengthens your Support Base, allowing you to be more competitive for future business. You now have a foothold in the account and begin the journey to displacing your competition!

This concludes our section on Value Creation. You are ready to learn how sales strategy packages politics and value to enable you to achieve relative superiority.

PART 4

STRATEGY

CHAPTER 11

INTRODUCTION TO COMPETE STRATEGY

All men can see these tactics whereby I conquer, but what none can see is the strategy out of which victory is evolved.

—Sun Tzu

You've now established your foundation of *Political Advantage* and *Value Creation* and are ready to enter the realm of compete sales strategy or, simply, *Compete Strategy*. The next few chapters brief you on how to use Compete Strategy as a way to outsell your competition by packaging politics, value, and Competitive Differentiation, thereby winning the business and best serving your customer.

WHAT IS COMPETE STRATEGY?

A Compete Strategy has one major job: to clearly and succinctly define what you are counting on to win a deal. It is a central organizing statement that enables you to make directionally correct decisions about what you will do in a sales campaign. Every tactic—everything you physically do— must directly or indirectly advance your Compete Strategy. The result is to create a nontraditional source of relative superiority—because most people are not strategic by nature. They cannot *see* it, which prevents them from *formulating* it.

For instance, spectators who did not know a lot about hockey and watched the underdog United States hockey team defeat the dominant Russians in the 1980 Olympics saw *tactics:* players skating around in circles with the puck and seemingly not taking a lot of shots at the goal. However, spectators with an advanced understanding of the game saw the US coach's brilliant and unexpected *strategy* of keeping the puck away from the Russians, which shifted the advantage to the smaller and better-conditioned US players and away from the larger and stronger Russian players.

Because most sellers don't possess this ability to *see* strategy, they remain uninformed spectators who aren't able to formulate strategy on their own. For this reason, they seldom deploy effective strategy even during the most competitive of sales situations. We observe this during deal reviews, when the majority of sellers answer our question "What is your strategy to win?" with either a blank stare or a 45-minute data dump of all their sales activity.

This is good news for you; you can hone the ability to see strategy by knowing what to look for. Once you can see it, you can then understand it. And when you understand it, you can then formulate and deploy it to great effect. Chapter 2 referred to advanced selling as a management science, one that is powerful. Here, you can further see why. As we make the intangibles of selling visible, it fosters understanding that, in turn, drives manageability and results. And all this is fundamentally based upon making the intangible tangible.

Strategy is intangible, as is the potential to move up the Sales Value Chain and create unexpected customer value. Also intangible is influence, which is seen only when it is exerted. But make no mistake; these intangibles are very real to the people involved.

- To the Fox who sees and understands influence, politics is a science.
- To the Stage IV Customer Advisor, who imagines the Unexpected Value that could be provided to a customer and what it looks like, the Sales Value Chain is as real as his or her commission check.
- This is all brought together in a most interesting and unconventional way to the strategist. To explain, let's leave selling for a moment.

Long narrow blades of grass that sway with the wind in a beautiful and delicate fashion grow in the wetlands of North America. If you were to reach out and grab a handful of this grass, it would break away easily; and if you tested the strength of any one blade, it would pull apart without effort. But if you were to take multiple blades of this grass and weave it together, it would support the weight of a full-grown person. One such blade of grass is influence, another is customer value, and still another is the product, along with total cost of ownership, company reputation, and so forth—all just blades of grass.

Strategy is what weaves these blades together to make the whole much stronger than its parts. Some of the blades are visible, like product, while others, such as influence, are not. And the weave itself is invisible to most. However, when we show you the four patterns that constitute strategy, you'll be able to see the intangible as tangible.

When you combine strategy with unexpected customer value, politics, and other *traditional* sources of relative superiority—like product—to form Compete Strategy, an invisible force multiplier emerges. This is a kind of asymmetric advantage, or level of competitive strength that is disproportionately greater than what would have been possible through traditional thinking alone. And this is what enables a new supplier to topple a strong incumbent. The relative superiority gained by Compete Strategy is, again, disproportionately greater than what would be *traditionally* possible. *How* you sell increases the value of *what* you sell.

When pursuing opportunities, there are four distinct classes of strategy that will represent your best chance of winning. Keep in mind, however, that vying for specific deals is not the only domain that requires good strategy. You may also apply the four classes to other goals and objectives, such as building a presence with customer senior management, solving particular customer problems, or advancing a key customer individual's Personal Motivator.

In short, if you need to accomplish something that is important yet challenging, it's time to formulate strategy.

Having said that, let's look at the four classes of Compete Strategy.

1. **Direct:** This is woven to be strong and requires that you meet the competition head-to-head. It is generally resource intense, predictable, and time sensitive. We often see installed incumbents deploy this within an account in an attempt to secure repeat business.
2. **Indirect:** Woven to be flexible, this takes place when you use unconventional thinking to change the ground rules, thereby catching the competition off guard in the 11th hour of a sales situation as it is peaking. We see this implemented in situations when a seller needs an asymmetric advantage, such as when a new supplier is challenging an incumbent who appears to be holding all the cards.
3. **Divisional:** This is where military strategy introduces deception to divide enemy forces; however, it is quite the opposite in selling. Woven to be tight and narrow, this approach allows you to *complement* the competition to *partition* the business. A close cousin to the Direct strategy, we see it deployed when the seller's Support Base is not adequate to support a Direct approach. Appropriately, the seller chooses to pursue only a part of the business, thus dividing the opportunity with other suppliers and gaining a foothold on which to build in the future.

4. **Containment:** Woven to be durable and long-lasting, this is the strategy to use when you feel that you cannot win a deal and need to buy more time in order to gain enough strength to change the ground rules and implement the Indirect approach.

As you examine these, you'll build an understanding of the conditions and circumstances that must exist for one to succeed. When certain conditions aren't present, you need to create them. For example, if you are going Direct and are in a position of strength, you need to collapse the sales cycle and close the deal. Time is not in your favor at that point, as circumstances beyond your control—such as a customer's reorganization—could easily derail you.

When you understand each strategy's strengths and weaknesses, you will be able to make rapid decisions about what *must* transpire in the sales cycle for you to win well before it comes to pass. At that point, deciding what tactics to use and in what sequence will be a natural, sensible, and creative process. You will come to better understand that tactics taken in the right sequence have a greater overall effect than if they are ordered in some other way. This will help you prioritize your sales activities when you are in the trenches of an important and highly competitive deal.

But first, remind yourself of what it really means to win. As you learned in Chapter 1, winning in sales is multi-dimensional; it involves the customer, the competition, and the supplier (you). The process of winning begins when a customer buys from you and not your competitors. But it doesn't *stop* there. The customer's decision to work with you must result in your improving his or her business in some way—increasing the customer's revenue and/or profits, for instance. Furthermore, this customer improvement must be in balance with some form of supplier improvement, either directly or in the future.

We all know of situations in which the seller will discount price or make resource commitments in the interest of winning business that will drive more profitable business in the long term. That's okay under the right circumstances, but *value* is not the sole property of the customer. It must be bilateral and balanced if a healthy relationship is to develop between the companies over time.

Stage IV Customer Advisors know this, which is evident when they negotiate a sale's terms and conditions after the decision has been made to go with them. Before negotiating, Customer Advisors have engaged in two key activities:

1. They will have had a discussion with the Situational Fox about key supplier considerations such as price, resource commitments,

payment terms, intellectual property rights, or other critical items. We cannot emphasize enough that negotiating with Procurement can be a nightmare if you haven't established an informal agreement in principle prior to that point with the Fox.

2. They know that their ability to protect the business integrity of a deal from their company's point of view will be only as good as the value they are providing to the customer. Put simply, Customer Advisors know that the higher you are on the Sales Value Chain, the easier it is to successfully negotiate a deal.

These two points create a negotiating platform, which is based on the following three considerations.

1. **Power Base Alignment:** It is absolutely critical that you construct your Value Statements and Value Propositions in collaboration with Power Base members and that your solution directly or indirectly advance the Personal Motivator of the Fox or other key people. You will recall this focus on politics in Chapters 3 through 7, in terms of developing *Political Advantage,* the first important competency that we introduced.

2. **Unexpected Customer Value:** It is equally important to utilize your political relationships to move up the Sales Value Chain to create as much business relevance as possible. Based on intel gathering and the support of the Power Base, this is the second important competency—*Value Creation,* presented in Chapters 8 through 10.

3. **Competitive Differentiation:** You must distinguish yourself from the competition and effectively communicate the advantage you bring to your customer. Although this third important sales competency is the subject of the next chapter, you have already begun to build differentiation in both *how* and *what* you sell. Most sellers, for example, do not master customer politics and align with Power Base members, which is part of *how* they sell. Nor do they create solutions that reside high on the Sales Value Chain, which is part of *what* they sell.

Next, we dive deep into Competitive Differentiation, a critical precursor to formulating sales strategy.

CHAPTER 12

COMPETITIVE DIFFERENTIATION

If you know the enemy and know yourself, your victory will not stand in doubt.
—Sun Tzu

To master Competitive Differentiation is to master the ability to gather competitive intel. This requires utilizing the intel-gathering process you learned in Chapter 6 and applying it to competitors by:

- Conducting *competitive* research.
- Making astute observations.
- Asking good questions.

We have observed how crucial the competitive intel-gathering process is during deal reviews. We often see a distinct lack of information about competitors, which ties a seller's hands when it comes to formulating strategy. In some cases, sellers are not even aware of the companies and individuals with whom they are competing while pursuing an important opportunity. This chapter examines what you need to know and how to find it through the process of research, observations, and questions. But in order to know the competition, you must first know yourself.

TO KNOW YOUR COMPETITION IS TO KNOW YOURSELF

Throughout this book, we have endeavored to equip you with an understanding of customer politics and value. However, as we dive into Competitive Differentiation, we must cover an issue that is totally in your hands.

You must know how your solution and company are differentiated from those of the competition in order to formulate a strategy, and strategy has but one purpose: to advance you to relative superiority in order to *win*. To do this, you need to not only possess a need to win but also must have a compelling need to *compete*. Stage III and IV sellers have both, whereas the 80 percent seller population in Stages I and II seek only to win.

The need to win without the will to compete is like a hungry person who is not willing to try something new.

This *will to compete* is a personal attribute of those sellers who are naturally inclined to want to do better than their adversaries. However, many sellers would prefer to win *without* the need to compete. These are sellers who are often referred to as "farmers," a familiar term that describes individuals who look after installed accounts. However, we think that *all* sellers in today's marketplace should possess more of a "hunter" mentality, since every account is subject to competitive displacement and every deal carries the risk of being outsold. Still, many sellers lack the will to compete, causing competition to become a blind spot in their selling efforts.

Since competitive ignorance has serious consequences, it is worth understanding. We have identified two contributing factors to this condition:

1. Many sellers view selling as a *focused activity between supplier and customer.* They therefore fail to consider competition and tend to believe in the numbers approach to generating business—that you will make quota if you make enough calls and uncover enough opportunities. These individuals focus on pipeline management, where numbers of unqualified leads develop into qualified leads that mature to a proposal phase and then into orders. This might have worked in days past, when one had a strong product in an up economy. However, those days are clearly behind us.

2. A smaller population of sellers truly believes that *they have no competition.* If they lose a deal, they will quickly tell you that it was due to price, a lack of product capability, or some other reason that was out of their control. These sellers propose a solution that competes with alternative solutions provided by other suppliers or the customer itself.

> For these sellers, the *solution* that they are proposing is in competition with alternative *solutions* provided by other suppliers or the customer itself. They don't view themselves as competing with other *sellers* because they cannot see the nontraditional sources of relative superiority, such as politics, unexpected customer value, and strategy, that they control.

Having worked with so many sellers over the last 30-plus years, we believe that sellers in both cases innately know that competition exists and that they should address it directly. But not everyone is wired to confront opposition in this way; most people don't take pleasure in benefiting directly at someone else's expense. At the same time, they are committed to their customers and, therefore, indirectly compete by outcaring and outservicing the competition. This is the archetype of the farmer.

We wish we could say that there is a place for such sellers—that if an account is large enough, it is wise to have both hunters and farmers on the account. But the truth is that these farmers are becoming less relevant in customers' eyes.

Customers Benefit Directly from Sellers Who Compete

It may be counterintuitive to some, but your will to compete will directly benefit your customer, because:

To compete is to move up the Sales Value Chain—and that produces significantly more value for your customer.

What does a seller's will to compete have to do with increasing customer value? It's hard work to move up the Sales Value Chain within an account; it takes time and effort that can come at the direct expense of other sales and sales support activities. It also requires executive-level expertise, as is seen with Stage IV Customer Advisors, which requires a developmental commitment on the part of most sellers.

What drives sellers who are *not* naturally competitive to make this investment when making quota is getting tougher and tougher each year? *It is the competition!* It's knowing that if they don't move north within an account, their risk of losing is significant. They're either more likely to be conventionally outsold or the competition will go north, thereby defeating them—often without their knowledge. Mastering the intangibles provides you with significant nontraditional sources of relative superiority and also makes it difficult for the competition to see what you are doing. If they can't see the intangibles, they likely cannot see you managing them.

Nothing produces more Competitive Differentiation than moving north up the Sales Value Chain and providing customers with the Unexpected Value that is the ultimate expression of outcaring the competition. As you do this, other suppliers who want to be competitive will ultimately have but one response: to do likewise. That means that:

> Customers will see a growing amount of value from suppliers over time, because the suppliers are demonstrating the will to compete! For this reason, it is paradoxical that sellers don't compete because they are focused on their customer and not their competitor. Yet, if they did compete, they would provide significantly more value to their customers. Such is the problem with the traditional thinking of the past.

Knowing Yourself

Almost all sellers will claim to compete; and in their minds, they truly do. But they often do not recognize that something else—something of which they aren't consciously aware—is taking place. At its core, the will to compete has the same quality that drives sellers to master the intangibles:

An offensive mind-set, which is defined as driving ambition tempered by humility

This attitude or orientation compels sellers to knock the ball out of the park when it comes to providing customers with Unexpected Value, while also taking advantage of a competitor's weaknesses without ever mentioning them.

The problem is that it is easy to labor under a *defensive* mind-set without knowing it, and this is what compels sellers to think that they're competing when they truly aren't. They rarely produce unexpected customer value because they believe that their job is to give the customer what he or she wants, which to them simply means being responsive. Even if the customer is wrong, they are hesitant to point this out for fear of damaging the relationship. Carry this defensive attitude a step further and we see that it spills over onto competitors. For example, if a customer individual is a Competitor Supporter, the defensive seller will tend not to call on him or her. The same goes for customer Opponents; Compete Strategy is a foreign language to these farmer-type sellers.

On the other hand, Stage III and IV sellers are assertive, innovative, and respectful but never arrogant toward customers. And they are equally assertive and innovative—but also professional—in the face of competition. They do not allow themselves to become overconfident in either situation. These sellers don't want to hurt their competition; they simply seek to defeat their competitor's sales strategy. For them, Compete Strategy is the intellectual sword of a sales campaign. It is an offensive mind-set that truly prepares you to take on the competition.

COMPETITIVE INTELLIGENCE GATHERING

Your competitive intel gathering begins with the horizontal axis of the Holden Four Stage Model. It is important to answer the four questions outlined in Figure 12.1 for each competitor your customer is evaluating.

Figure 12.1
Competitive Intel

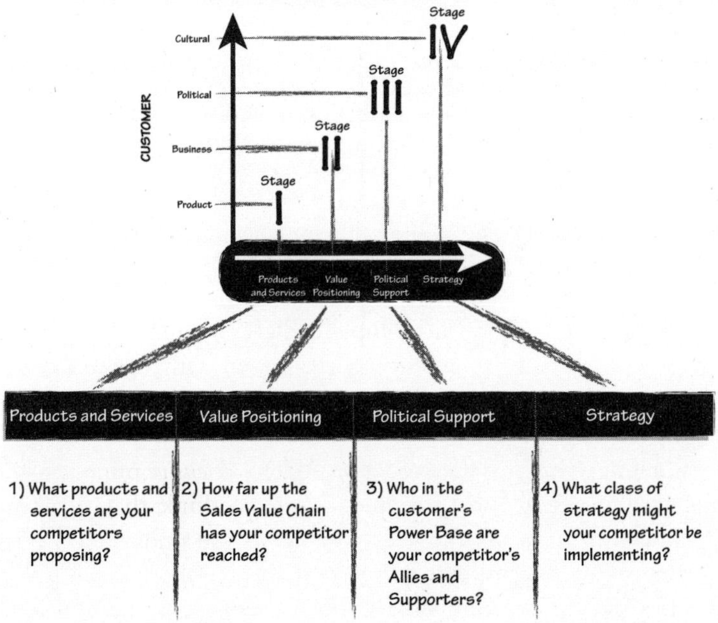

Stage IV
Cultural
Stage III
Political
CUSTOMER
Stage II
Business
Stage I
Product
Products and Services
Value Positioning
Political Support
Strategy
Products and Services
Value Positioning
Political Support
Strategy
1) What products and services are your competitors proposing?
2) How far up the Sales Value Chain has your competitor reached?
3) Who in the customer's Power Base are your competitor's Allies and Supporters?
4) What class of strategy might your competitor be implementing?

The intel that you gather in this exercise will help you build a Compete Strategy by first:

- Knowing what solution your competition is proposing.
- Knowing how that solution's value is positioned on the Sales Value Chain.

Figure 12.2
Competitive Intel—Expanded

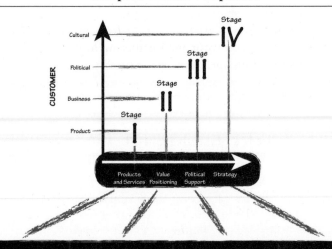

Products and Services	Value Positioning	Political Support	Strategy
1) What products and services are your competitors proposing?	2) How far up the Sales Value Chain has your competitor reached?	3) Who in the customer's Power Base are your competitor's Allies and Supporters?	4) What class of strategy might your competitor be implementing?
A. What are the strengths and weaknesses?	A. What do customers tend to value?	A. Who do they generally call on in accounts?	A. What class of strategy have you seen to be successful?
B. What industries do they target?	B. Who are their largest customers?	B. Who do they focus their marketing on?	B. What is their company business strategy? Performance?

SOURCES

- ✓ Your customer contacts
- ✓ Alliance partner organizations selling to same customers
- ✓ Third-party consultants or industry analysts
- ✓ Evaluating your competitor's product/service through personal use, webinars, and industry conferences
- ✓ Customer case studies on your competitor's website
- ✓ Astute observation by your extended sales team
- ✓ Sellers in your company who have faced the same competitor in other accounts
- ✓ Networking with noncompeting sellers who sell to the same customer industry
- ✓ Competitor's Annual Report and presentations
- ✓ Competitor's website and press releases

- Knowing whether the competition has gotten to the Situational Fox ahead of you—and, if not, the individuals with whom they are aligned in terms of the Power Base.
- Discovering what class of strategy the competitor is most likely implementing. This is where your intel gathering looks back into history. Most suppliers who experience success will repeat the sales strategy that helped them gain that success, so keep track of what your major competitors have done before.

You will notice that you transition from the tangible to the intangible as you move from left to right in Figure 12.1. This movement suggests that most sellers are more comfortable focusing on product and services than on sales strategy. To help you gather critical competitive intel, particularly as you move to the right and into the intangibles, Figure 12.2 identifies what information is essential, along with where you can find it.

Although you can never have enough intel, having the time to gather it is an issue for many sellers. Remember to keep in mind the process that you learned in Chapter 6 regarding research, observations, and questions. The principles are the same, but implementation differs to some degree.

Two major principles apply when you are gathering competitive intel:

1. Keep the questions you ask about the competition tightly focused and recognize that asking *closed* questions is appropriate and necessary. "Tightly focused" questions are halfway between open and closed. An open-ended question might be, "What is my competition proposing?" A tighter question would be, "What is it about my competitor's solution that you find interesting?" This allows you to hone in on a subset of the competitor's solution—not the whole thing, since it is much easier to get people to disclose information in small amounts at a time. Feel free to repeat questions after the customer individual responds, such as, "Is there anything else you find interesting or of value?"

   Closed questions are also appropriate, even at the beginning of the dialog when you are determining where to focus your questions. A simple but essential question could be, "Who is my competitor?" You want to orient your inquiries to the closed question end of the continuum when focusing on competitive intel. This is the opposite of what you should do when gathering customer information and working on the open question end of the continuum, as shown in Figure 12.3.

Figure 12.3
Gathering Intel

2. Keep your dialog casual and informal, and interact with only one person at a time—not with multiple customer individuals, and *never* in a formal business meeting.

Here are a few practical tips about where to find competitive intel, based on the sources outlined in Figure 12.2:

- **Your customer contacts.** Speak with customer individuals involved in the buying decision or those who are likely to know what the competition is up to, such as Allies, Supporters, and Non-Supporters. You will be surprised by how many people will simply tell you what you want to know. Allies and Supporters in particular may share valuable insight if they believe it will enhance the value that you can give their company.
- **Alliance partner organizations selling to the same customer.** Talking to alliance partners who are engaged with the customer will augment your intel. Look for ways to provide partners with value in order to encourage them to share their insights with you. In return, be generous in providing them with insight, but do not disclose anything that could compromise your standing with the customer.
- **Evaluating your competitor's product through webinars and industry conferences.** Firsthand observations provide rich insight into the type of value a competitor can provide. Keep in mind, however, that you will need insight from customer individuals to determine where they are on the Sales Value Chain.
- **Customer case studies on your competitor's website.** You can gain a lot of insight—such as the size of your competitor's typical customer, their industry expertise, and product differentiation—by assessing case studies. Also, seeing who (in terms of role) from the customer's organization is quoted in the case study—whether he or she is in operations, middle management, or at the executive level—will provide clues as to the level of customer penetration that exists.
- **Astute observations by your extended sales team.** Familiarize your team with the value of asking questions to gather

competitive intel. It's helpful to role-play this with them so that they can become comfortable with the approach.

- **Sellers in your company who have faced the same competitor in other accounts.** Past behavior is a great indicator of future behavior.
- **Networking with noncompeting sellers who sell to the same customer industry.** Other sellers are a great source of insight because they see a lot, like to talk, and are inclined to want to help a fellow seller. Remember to return the favor and help them whenever you can. Guard against being viewed as a fair weather friend.
- **Competitor's Annual Report and presentations.** Your competitor's company strategy will influence its sales strategies in the field. Let's say that your customer wants an on-premise software solution and your competitor's Chief Executive Officer (CEO) recently stated that the company's strategy is to migrate all products to the public cloud. Consider whether this could be a point of vulnerability for you to exploit.
- **Competitor's website and press releases.** Yet another way to determine who your competitor's sales campaigns consider important is to read about their marketing campaigns, which often name specific industries. Who is your competitor's primary audience in their website layout and messaging?

COMPETITIVE DIFFERENTIATION ANALYSIS

Armed with this competitive information, you are ready to run what we call a Competitive Differentiation Analysis, which will identify your strengths and weaknesses against those of your competition. Your focus here will shift from gathering *information* to developing competitive *insight*—specifically, determining where you and the competition are both vulnerable when considering product, value, politics, and strategy.

The most dangerous strategic condition exists when a supplier is vulnerable but unaware of it. This should prompt you to identify your own weaknesses that you may not be aware of, while also seeking to identify competitive weakness. In addition, you will identify your strengths against those of your competition with the intent of fully leveraging yours and be able to sidestep the competition.

The Competitive Differentiation Analysis is a matrix with four quadrants, as shown in Figure 12.4.

Figure 12.4
The Competitive Differentiation Analysis

The *Maintain* box in the upper left quadrant shows the strengths you share with your competitor. For example, if an individual in the customer's Power Base perceives that both your own and your competitor's products are reliable, then reliability is not a point of differentiation for either of you. This quadrant is so labeled because you want to sustain the customer's perception that you meet this buying criterion.

The *Explore* box in the lower right quadrant is where you record weaknesses that exist for both you and your competitor—again, per the customer's judgment. For example, let's say that the customer wants to integrate with their billing system—something that neither you nor your competition can accomplish. You would then note "lack of integration" as an entry to Explore. Depending on the business and political significance of this buying criterion, you may decide to not address it. Or, you might dive into developing a way to meet the criterion in a manner that moves it to the upper right *Attack* quadrant.

The lower left quadrant is the *Defend* box, where you identify your competitor's strengths that you cannot directly match. These are the points of vulnerability that you will have to manage during your sales campaign by formulating a Compete Strategy that shifts the weighting of the buying criteria away from them. For example, if you know that the price of your competitor's solution is 20 percent lower than yours, you may need to shift the focus to total cost of ownership or sidestep the issue with offsetting customer Unexpected Value to justify the increased price. Although these issues reside within the Defend box, the key is not to be defensive about them. You defend by justifying or minimizing the importance of the issue from the customer's point of view.

Finally, there is the *Attack* box in the upper right quadrant—your strengths that your competitor cannot match and points of Competitive Differentiation. For example, if the Situational Fox prioritizes working with a supplier with a track record of large deployments in a specific industry, which you have and your competitor does not, then you may choose to make this one of your Attack points that your Compete Strategy emphasizes. You accomplish this by fully characterizing the customer value associated with the strength.

Run this analysis for each of your competitors and even potential competitors that are not currently present but that could surface late in the sales cycle. It is also critical that you:

- Focus your efforts on insight that is **specific to the customer deal** you are trying to win, rather than broad market assumptions.
- Complete the analysis **from the perspective of your customer's Power Base.** For example, if you believe that your product is faster but no one in the customer's Power Base considers speed to be part of their buying criteria, then you are not ready to include it as an Attack point.
- Pay particular attention to the **Attack and Defend boxes,** as they tell the story when it comes to differentiation, as shown in Figure 12.5.

Figure 12.5
Attack and Defend Boxes

You want to positively distance yourself from the competition as much as possible. When you are both strong or both weak in the same box, you are essentially "sitting next to each other." When you are strong and the competition is weak, you are ahead; but when you are weak and the competition is strong, you are behind. Compete Strategy is all about disproportionately moving out ahead of the competition. To get an operational handle on this, we recommend that you *score* the Attack and Defend boxes and analyze it graphically. For example, for every entry identified in each box, score its customer relevance from the point of view of the Situational Power Base. If:

- Relevance is high, give it 3 points.
- It is important, but not critical, give it 2 points.
- It is not important, give it 1 point.
- You don't know, apply a default score of 1 if in the Attack box and 3 if in the Defend box.

Then subtract the Defend total from the Attack total to calculate your score. To determine the competitor's score, subtract the Attack total from the Defend total. For example, let's say that your Attack points equaled 2 and your Defend points equaled 4 compared to a key competitor. Your net score is −2, while your competitor's score is +2. You can see that you are behind when you look at it graphically, as shown in Figure 12.6.

Figure 12.6
Scoring the Competitive Differentiation Analysis

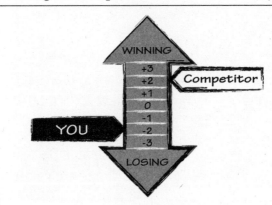

Keep in mind that the earlier you can do this in the sales cycle, the better. If you don't know something, the fact that you know that you don't know it is an astute observation in your intel gathering, which will lead you to ask good questions. Don't get caught up trying to label something as a 1 or 2, or a 2 or 3; just keep it simple. You're looking for big gaps between the Attack and Defend box scores. And if they don't exist, you need to create them with the right Compete Strategy.

Quantifying your differentiation analysis will remove a lot of the subjectivity, enable you to compare your compete position relative to specific competitors, and observe how those positions change over time. Perhaps more important, it will help you formulate the actual Compete Strategy to win a particular deal by more clearly seeing the weave of strategy—and the blades of grass that compose it.

As this is a Stage IV exercise, our data tell us that, conservatively, 80 percent or more of the seller population will have no clue what you are doing. They cannot manage what they cannot see, which will provide you with a nontraditional source of relative superiority.

We start operationalizing this thinking in the next chapter, as we return to the four classes of Compete Strategy in more depth, starting with the *Direct* approach.

CHAPTER 13

THE DIRECT STRATEGY

TRADITIONAL AND NONTRADITIONAL APPLICATION

The truly wise can perceive things before they have come to pass.

—Sun Tzu

The most common strategy employed in selling is the *Direct* approach. This occurs when you go head-to-head against the competition, matching your strength against theirs in what is really a battle for relative superiority. Whoever has it when the sales situation peaks wins. However, if you achieve this superiority too early—before the customer is ready, willing, and able to make a purchase decision—you lose. But achieve it too late, and you also lose.

Most sellers use this as their default strategy. They are drawn to the tangible—product, features and benefits, price, and so on, rather than invisible intangibles such as politics, value, and strategy. However, they often don't even know that they are deploying a *Direct* strategy. This—combined with the fact that they aren't able to see and understand strategy—keeps them from recognizing the timing dynamic mentioned previously.

For example, let's say that a Stage II Solution Seller who is an incumbent supplier with an installed base is competing for a repeat purchase. He instinctively puts as much traditional value in front of the customer as possible early in the sales cycle. But the Stage IV Customer Advisor, who also wants the business, instead finds ways to delay the decision, therefore buying time to launch a sales campaign of invisibles that leverages politics, value, and strategy. Using the *Containment* strategy that we introduced in Chapter 11, this seller achieves two critical task objectives. First, she has forced the incumbent to *peak too early,* which means that he has only one direction to go: down. It is simply too difficult to hold a position of relative superiority for very long.

Every sales cycle will peak at some point, and when it does, you will find yourself in an unstable state.

Peaking occurs when certain events or circumstances converge that cause the customer to be ready, willing, and able to make a purchase decision. Perhaps funding has just been approved, the Fox has made his views clear to the people conducting the evaluation, it is the end of the quarter, or so on. Whatever the reason, a decision must be made in what is often an emotionally charged environment. Decision makers are concerned about the potential impact of a decision on their careers or on their bonus. And, on top of that, the weighting of the decision-making criteria is generally subjective.

All of this adds up to an unstable situation, not unlike that of nature, which is subject to the second law of thermodynamics. It states that differences in the parameters that characterize a closed or isolated system (a sales situation)—like that which causes a customer to be ready, willing, and able to make a decision—will and must *equilibrate,* or attain a state of equilibrium. In other words, the factors that cause a sales situation to peak must normalize as quickly as they are able. The funding is pulled away, the Fox exits the Situational Power Base, the quarter ends—take your pick. But eventually, the second law of thermodynamics will apply, eliminating your ability to close the deal.

That means that a seller implementing a *Direct* strategy may have relative superiority at one point and not the next. So it is helpful to *know* and sometimes *influence* when a sales situation is peaking, and it is important to be prepared to capitalize on it. The best way to do both is to observe a sales situation through the lens of strategy. What can appear as insignificant customer or competitive events may take on tremendous importance when sellers view them within the context of strategy, as you will see in this and the next chapters. Keep the following in mind as you make your way through them:

Strategy is the key to understanding the dynamics of any competitive sales campaign. The key to strategy is making the invisible intangibles visible—which you can achieve through unconventional thinking and adopting an offensive mind-set.

Let's return to our example of the seller who is using the *Containment* strategy. In addition to forcing the incumbent to *peak too early,* the seller achieves a second critical task objective: getting stronger as the incumbent gets weaker. She will go Fox Hunting and determine how to move up the Sales Value Chain to provide the customer with Unexpected Value, which will more than offset any compatibility or financial issues associated with switching suppliers. She will simultaneously formulate strategy, likely selecting the *Indirect* approach that we explore further in Chapter 14.

Without question, there are times when a *Direct* strategy is appropriate in selling, notably when the following two conditions exist, which are based on tangible and intangible sources of relative superiority:

- Your Attack box is aligned with the customer's buying criteria, as viewed by the Situational Power Base.
- Your Attack box is significantly greater than your Defend box.

Most often, these conditions exist when you:

- **Are the installed incumbent** and counting on your installed base to create barriers to entry for the competition, along with a strong Support Base and a history of providing unexpected customer value.
- **Have a category killer product,** meaning you can rely on being the only game in town or on having moved high up on the Sales Value Chain in the past.
- **Are "selling the company,"** which means you can leverage the value of your company's resident body of expertise, its solution flexibility, and its dedication to customers in the form of:
  - **Understanding** the customer, the industry, and the needs that the supplier meets.
  - **Commitment** to fulfill and exceed those needs whenever possible.
  - **Ability** to put forth a clear demonstration of the resources necessary to ensure fulfillment and success.

So let's explore these sales scenarios from a traditional and nontraditional point of view, where the traditional sources of superiority that drive the *Direct* strategy are foundational and the nontraditional sources are incremental. The first is one that we have already touched on: being an installed incumbent.

WHEN YOU ARE THE INSTALLED INCUMBENT

Traditional Sources

The most common expression of the *Direct* strategy involves situations where you already have a strong presence in an account. As new sales opportunities arise with the customer, you may be able to gain relative superiority simply because of the strength of your installation, even if your products have begun to lag somewhat in sophistication and capability. For example, if you are selling business intelligence (BI) software to a customer who already uses your Customer Resource Management (CRM) system, you'll have an advantage if the two integrate effortlessly. The customer will probably want to avoid spending time and money on a new system that might not integrate as well with the existing one.

Two things must be true for this version of the *Direct* strategy to work: First, the customer individuals must be satisfied with the product or service they've already received from you. Second, customer individuals must conclude, perhaps reluctantly, that their attraction to another supplier isn't worth the drawbacks of having a multi-supplier environment. If it's a toss-up, your presence in the account shouldn't lull you into thinking you have an edge. Again, this is the traditional perspective, one that doesn't account for the invisible factors.

Nontraditional Sources

Here, the barriers to entry go beyond the traditional view to include Unexpected Value that sits high up on the Sales Value Chain and has the support of the Situational Power Base. These nontraditional sources of relative superiority, on top of the traditional sources, make the *Direct* strategy viable.

WHEN YOU HAVE A CATEGORY KILLER PRODUCT

Traditional Sources

We also see people who are selling a truly unique item that is a category killer employ the *Direct* strategy. These are products whose launch creates an entirely new market. Companies that sell these innovative products use their first mover advantage and brand identity to keep competitors at bay initially, which allows them to build significant market share. Examples of such products include:

- Google's Internet advertising and search offering
- Oracle's relational database
- Microsoft's personal computer Windows operating system and Office applications (Word, Excel, PowerPoint)
- Apple's iPod, iPhone, and iPad—and before that, the Sony Walkman

Sometimes, category killer products transform their companies' name into verbs, such as, "Could you please *Xerox* the form for me?" or "Just *Google* it if you need driving directions." A company's name slips into general usage when at some point their product is seen as having exclusive ownership of the market. Although it may only be a matter of perception, the fact remains that while these perceptions exist, these companies enjoy an enormous competitive advantage. There is no better type of product superiority like being perceived to be the only game in town. But how often is this really the case? Other suppliers eventually catch up, making this strategy increasingly less successful for most sellers.

Nontraditional Sources

The traditional perspective focuses on physical product superiority, but the nontraditional view leverages the human expertise and thought leadership that is required to go north in an account and then connect Unexpected Value to the advancement of a Fox's Personal Motivator. This combines human and product strength to support a *Direct* approach.

WHEN YOU ARE SELLING THE COMPANY

Traditional Sources

Although selling the company is part of every sales campaign, it becomes the key focus at times—more important than depending on the product or solution to carry the day. This truly means selling the value of the relationship with a specific supplier, which can easily eclipse feature-and-benefit value or the reduced price of any one product as part of any one sales situation. It is all about the aggregate total value of advancing a customer's business over time—and it's where supplier expertise, resources, and dedication to customers can be powerful, albeit still traditional. When a customer individual tells you that "No one ever got fired by selecting Company X," you know that company has achieved this kind of market reputation superiority. Firms like McKinsey & Company and IBM have so distinguished themselves.

Nontraditional Sources

Whereas the focus of the traditional view is on the relationship between the companies—supplier and customer—the nontraditional perspective centers on the relationship between a Customer Advisor and Power Base members, which brings us back to people. This is why a supplier's Customer Advisors are an essential source of relative superiority.

Sellers implement the *Direct* strategy in many more types of sales scenarios than those identified previously. Its common use would be less of a problem if more sellers met the Competitive Differentiation Analysis conditions mentioned earlier. This would force them to focus on nontraditional thinking and the invisible intangibles of politics, Unexpected Value, and strategy, along with more of an offensive mind-set—but they usually do not. So what does all this mean? Ironically, the most appropriate time to use the *Direct* strategy is when you don't need it. But if you combine the traditional and nontraditional sources of relative superiority and you manage the timing well, the *Direct* strategy can be effective.

Viewed differently, the *Direct* approach may also make sense if you are competing with someone who has only traditional sources of superiority, while you have the invisible intangibles on your side.

GETTING THE TIMING RIGHT

If you have the product, company, or installed base superiority to go *Direct,* with both the tangible and intangible sources of relative superiority, it is important to carefully manage the timing of the close as much as you can. You must avoid peaking too early or too late. The sales situation peaks when the customer buyers are:

- **Ready:** They've assessed all competitive alternatives and need to make a decision due to business, financial, political, or supplier incentive reasons. We refer to this need as a *driving mechanism.*
- **Willing:** They've communicated with the customer's Situational Power Base and the necessary level of executive/management, who will support a particular decision.
- **Able:** They've secured the necessary funding.

As a supplier, you can influence all these customer states in the following manner:

- **Ready:** Be responsive to the customer while aligning the decision-making criteria around your strengths, as in the Attack box of the Competitive Differentiation Analysis. In addition, advance the Situational Fox's Personal Motivator and provide appropriate incentives to the customer, such as enhanced service support if a decision is made within a certain period.
- **Willing:** Align with the Situational Fox and other Power Base members.
- **Able:** Provide Unexpected Value to overjustify an acquisition.

This influence is what can potentially allow you to have impact when a sales situation peaks. You can often discern the probable close date of a sales opportunity, but that is not always accurate and delays are inevitable.

The ability to influence the close date, and work your strategy to peak coincident to that date, is essential to the effective deployment of strategy.

THE DIRECT STRATEGY STATEMENT

You must be able to clearly and succinctly state your strategy, since this explains how you will leverage both traditional and nontraditional sources of relative superiority to win, while also providing directional guidance throughout the sales campaign. A complex or convoluted strategy will not serve this most important purpose. As such, the key elements to a *Direct* strategy statement include:

- The class of strategy.
- The critical customer business focus, such as some aspect of unexpected customer value.
- The critical political focus such as on a Fox who has a specific Personal Motivator.
- Unexpected or discounted competitor vulnerability, such as the overconfidence of an installed supplier or a weakness in solution capability, as it relates to providing value higher up on the Sales Value Chain.
- The timing, in terms of when you want the sales situation to peak and close.

Together, these elements not only provide a strategy statement but also convey a theme for the entire sales campaign, against which you can then judge all future activities and developments. An example of such a *Direct* strategy statement is the following:

> Our *Direct* approach is to meet all customer requirements, while also providing Unexpected Value in the area of manufacturing throughput, advancing the corporation's growth goal and the Fox's Personal Motivator of winning the current Power Struggle within Manufacturing, which is time sensitive, thus peaking the sales situation at the end of November.

A general template to assist you with this consists of the tool in Figure 13.1.

Figure 13.1
***Direct* Strategy Statement Template**

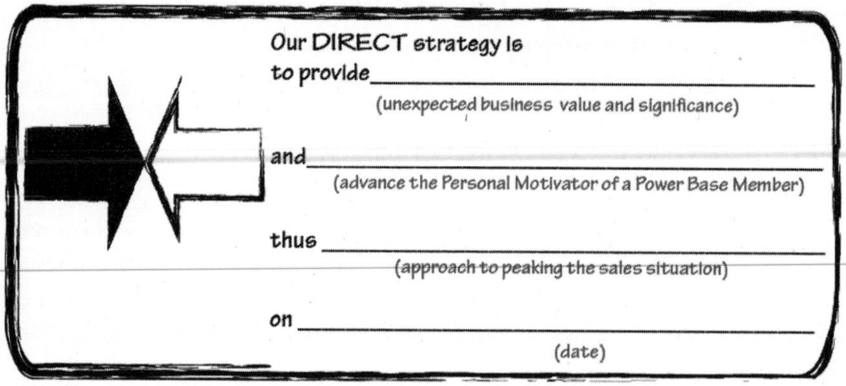

```
Our DIRECT strategy is
to provide_____
              (unexpected business value and significance)

and_____
          (advance the Personal Motivator of a Power Base Member)

thus _____
               (approach to peaking the sales situation)

on _____
                        (date)
```

CONCLUSION

Sales strategy is the intellectual sword of your sales campaign, thus making the *Direct* strategy like a *bronze* sword. It is better than no strategy, but even with a bronze sword, you are using seventh century BC technology. Better is not the *iron* sword of the eighth century BC, but rather its technologically advanced offspring—the stronger, sharper, and more resilient *steel* sword that is the subject of our next chapter, the *Indirect* strategy.

CHAPTER 14

THE INDIRECT STRATEGY

CHANGING THE GROUND RULES

Appear where you are not expected.

—Sun Tzu

Stage IV Customer Advisors know that it is uncommon for sellers to marshal all the traditional and nontraditional sources of relative superiority necessary at a specific and early point in the sales cycle. For this reason, Customer Advisors focus on the *Indirect* strategy as the intellectual sword of their sales campaign; it produces the highest win rates of any class of strategy. It accomplishes this by leveraging politics, unexpected customer value, and strategy to shape the customer's buying criteria.

With an Indirect strategy, you work to change the ground rules by which your customer will make a decision. You identify unexpected customer value in your Attack box and work with the customer Power Base to make this the primary buying criteria for the decision.

The element of *timing* is critically important with the *Indirect* approach, in terms of:

- **Upfront Speed:** It requires that you quickly identify unexpected customer value and align it with the Situational Power Base early in the sales cycle. This will help you establish an informal agreement in principle with the Power Base in terms of what unexpected customer value you'll provide—and when during the sales cycle.
- **Back-end Surprise:** It requires that the seller hold back on proposing Unexpected Value to a customer until a specific point late in the sales cycle. This enables you to pull the rug out from under your competitors at a point when they have little chance to catch up.

Now, let's take a moment to take a look at different types of competitive ways the *Indirect* strategy has been implemented.

CHANGING THE GROUND RULES

History is full of examples of how changing the ground rules enabled a seemingly weaker opponent to win a surprise outcome. Think about the American Revolution and what the superior British considered the rules to be. They expected to wage the conflict according to custom. Well-trained, immaculately uniformed troops from both sides would make a broad-daylight march in precise columns to an open field. It would be an orderly affair. After soldiers in one row fired, they would reload from a crouch to allow troops behind them a clear shot at the enemy. At the end, whichever side's troops were still standing would be the winner.

It didn't take George Washington and the Americans long to figure out that a battle of attrition made no sense. They were a small force taking on a world power. But what they did have was the ability to think unconventionally, as well as the will to win and compete—an offensive mind-set that existed in sharp contrast to that of the British, who unknowingly labored under a defensive mind-set that was steeped in tradition.

To succeed, Washington needed an asymmetric advantage—and the best way to achieve this was by changing the ground rules with an *Indirect* strategy.

Instead of an open-field *Direct* approach, the Americans launched a guerrilla effort; they engaged in nighttime operations and ambushed the British with mobility and the element of surprise. Sabotage and snipers who specifically targeted British officers added insult to injury. Because this counterintuitive American approach made the British so indignant, they were slow and ineffective in responding—and the rest, of course, is history.

Just as the Americans forced the British to fight an unconventional guerrilla war on unfriendly wooded terrain, the Stage IV Customer Advisor forces his or her competitors into a similar set of adverse circumstances by changing the ground rules. Although the mission, environment, and time in history are very different, the same principles apply, as you can see in this next sales example.

LEVERAGING POLITICS, UNEXPECTED VALUE, AND STRATEGY TO SHAPE THE CUSTOMER'S BUYING CRITERIA

Let's say that you sell automatic teller machine (ATM) equipment and are attempting to win an opportunity at a commercial bank with multiple branches. The installed incumbent is your primary competitor. The bank is not totally unhappy with your competitor, but it has decided to bid it out due to concerns about service and a desire to test the market for lower prices. The bank's Facilities Department was in charge of the bid and their request for proposal (RFP) stated the buying criteria as price, reliability/uptime, and service—the same criteria they used in a previous evaluation.

You quickly gather intel and conduct a preliminary Competitive Differentiation Analysis to see where you stand, as is shown in Figure 14.1.

Figure 14.1
Example of Your Competitive Differentiation Analysis

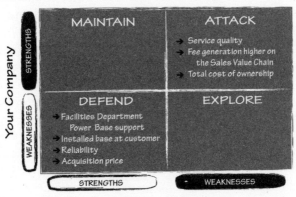

It is no surprise that your Defend box shows that you are not the installed incumbent and lack the support of the Facilities Department's Power Base. You also recognize that your competitor's equipment scores high in reliability/uptime, and it has a lower price. All in all, your competitor looks to offer a good solution—that is, on the surface.

But a different kind of picture emerges as you shift your attention to your Attack box. Your service quality is above industry standards. This is particularly important given the sophistication of your newest product, which provides capabilities such as bill payment. This enables the bank to generate fees, thereby producing new revenue and a potential source of Unexpected Value that could move you north on the Sales Value Chain. And although this comes at a higher price, the customer's total cost of ownership (TCO) would actually be *lower* than that of their existing installation.

This looks encouraging, and it might be enough for many sellers to launch a *Direct* campaign. But that is only a surface view of the situation. A more rigorous and objective look shows that the way you consider the Attack and Defend box entries could potentially make each stronger than the other. However, there is no overwhelming difference as they sit now in terms of relative superiority.

This is where the offensive mind-set kicks in. The first intellectual foundation of morale is being confident that you can win. *The will to win and compete is the belief that you can win!* And so you know that if a Fox or Power Base member sees the points in your Attack box as important, that person will likely become the customer's primary decision criteria.

If the ratio of Attack to Defend was 1:1 before, it is now something like 3:1. Not because service fee income and TCO are necessarily three times more important than reliability and price, but because the Fox *judges* them to be more important—which gives you disproportionate competitive advantage. Therefore, a $(1 + Fox):1 = 3:1$, in terms of competitive advantage equivalency. Now, let's look at how this might play out politically.

You apply your Fox-Hunting skills to first map out the Facilities Department's Power Base. Your intel suggests that this group has the authority and influence to make the buying decision as the ground rules are currently defined, because these are the same people who made the previous purchase decision. On further investigation, you determine that although they do care about service, their primary focus is really on lowering the price and increasing uptime. Additional intel would seem to suggest that your competitor is calling on only the Facilities Department. You recognize that to reprioritize the buying criteria to fee generation and TCO, you will need a champion with enough influence to intervene.

Therefore, you apply the account penetration process learned in Chapter 10 to determine that the head of retail banking is in the Enterprise Power Base. You approach him with a Value Statement based on fee generation that supports his critical business issue of creating new revenue sources to fuel growth. Here, you are developing two *Indirect* strategy force multipliers:

1. You identify a Fox powerful enough to intervene and alter how the buying criteria are weighted. The retail banking Fox is part of the Enterprise Power Base in this example, so he has enough influence to reprioritize the Facilities Department's buying criteria. Of course, he will do this in a foxlike manner, likely behind the scenes and through other people. To help ensure that the Fox will want to intervene, you also think about how to advance his Personal Motivator. In this case, it is to provide him with increased credibility to support his Power Struggle with commercial lending for funding so that he can expand retail banking as a core growth strategy for the organization. It is all this that, again, provides you with a 3:1 competitive advantage equivalency. But there is still one more force multiplier to go—and that centers on value.

2. You must move up the Sales Value Chain to create Unexpected Value for the customer. You are moving north from providing expected value of ATMs to the Facilities Department (which your solution addresses) to also providing Unexpected Value by significantly advancing the corporate goal of increasing revenue growth.

Now, the combination of political leverage and Unexpected Value gives you a competitive advantage equivalency ratio of something like 6:1, which shows genuine relative superiority.

This example represents the kind of strategic thinking that is critical in today's competitive selling. Again, it all hinges on the three invisibles: politics, value, and strategy. Pivotal to leveraging these three invisibles, however, is a very important tactical consideration when deploying both the *Indirect* and *Direct* strategies.

ESTABLISHING THE PRIME OBJECTIVE

The Prime Objective of a sales campaign is not the sales objective of securing an order for a particular solution by a specific point in time. Yet, it is just as important.

The Prime Objective is an accomplishment that, when achieved, will directly lead to relative superiority—the point in a sales cycle when you have gained a decisive advantage over the competition. When you can sustain that superiority, you exponentially increase the likelihood of closing the deal. If you lose it, however, it is very difficult to regain.

In our Revolutionary War example, the equivalent to the Prime Objective was giving France the confidence in the American cause that it needed to enter the war as an American ally—which America achieved in October 1777. Victory at the Battle of Saratoga gave the Americans relative superiority that they sustained with French military and financial assistance. It was the turning point of the war!

Another example of a Prime Objective is seen with mountain climbers. In Figure 14.2, you see a point in the climb that, when successfully achieved, suggests that the summit will surely follow.

Figure 14.2
Achieving the Prime Objective

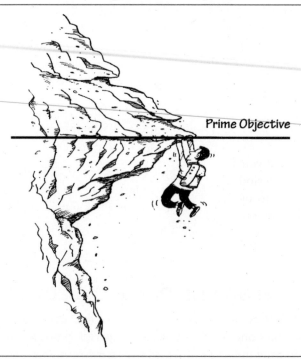

For example, when climbing Mount Kilimanjaro in East Africa, *mission success* is achieved by reaching the summit at 19,340 feet above sea level and returning safely to base camp. On the final ascent to the summit lies the Prime Objective.

At 15,500 feet sits Barafu Camp, a launch point to the summit. At midnight, teams begin the climb from Barafu to the crater rim. If a team reaches approximately 17,000 feet at or about the time the sun comes up, they will likely make the summit. Arrive at that point too early and the pace of the team may be too quick, causing some climbers to experience exhaustion too early in the summit attempt. Arrive too late and the team may not reach the summit early enough in the day to be safe given changing weather conditions.

In a competitive sales campaign, the Prime Objective, or turning point, needs to be accomplished early in the sales cycle. The Prime Objective was achieved in our ATM example when you developed insight into how to provide the unexpected business value of new revenue generation and shared that insight with the retail banking Business Unit Fox. That was the point at which the ground rules changed.

However, the beauty is that no one was aware of this change. The Facilities Department and your competitor were not yet in the loop. Only later when your proposal included an alternative recommendation that the retail banking Fox endorsed did everyone begin to see the changing landscape of the sales situation. Catching your competitor off guard and scrambling, as well as utilizing proper Fox-to-Fox connectivity between retail banking and facilities, you realized victory in a way that pleased everybody involved—except your competitor.

If you're selling to government, you know how difficult it can be once you are working under strict procurement rules and procedures, like Federal Acquisition Regulations (FAR) in the United States. As such, it is even more critical that you achieve your Prime Objective early, before you enter that restrictive period. Only then will you have enhanced access to people and be able to operate in a more exploratory fashion to discover the potential to create unexpected customer value and align yourself politically. Winning the battle before it is fought applies to all forms of competition— no matter what the endeavor.

MILESTONE STACKING

A core element to achieving a Prime Objective as early as possible in a sales campaign is Milestone Stacking. This is a critical implementation vehicle for establishing the upfront speed necessary for the *Indirect* approach.

Milestone Stacking means accomplishing multiple task objectives simultaneously or nearly simultaneously. The closer these task objectives are to each other in time, the more the synergy exists between them. In other words, maximum synergy or potentiation (the 1 + 1 = 3 phenomenon) occurs when you achieve critical task objectives in parallel. The result is to geometrically increase win potential and decrease competitive vulnerability, which you can see graphically in Figure 14.3.

Figure 14.3
The Impact of Milestone Stacking

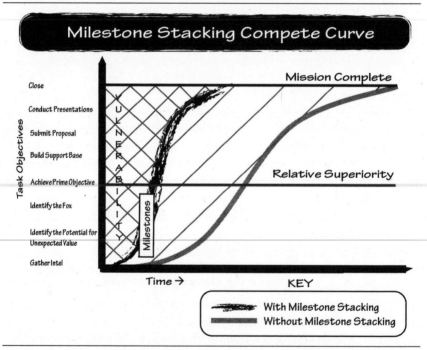

Note: The Milestone Stacking diagram is based on a military version presented by William H. McRaven in his book *Spec Ops* (Novato, CA: Presidio Press, 1995).

Milestone Stacking will shape the trajectory of the compete curve. The heavily drawn line in Figure 14.3 illustrates the impact of Milestone Stacking, in contrast to the lighter curve with no Stacking. You'll note that:

- You can achieve relative superiority much sooner with Stacking, as it dramatically shortens the sales cycle.

- Stacking geometrically reduces competitive vulnerability, while disproportionately increasing win potential; the two go hand-in-hand.
- If you delay in achieving the Prime Objective by, say $2\times$, your competitive vulnerability will increase by $4\times$. This makes time a constitutive factor, as important as the solution itself.
- The sales activity level is highest very early in the sales cycle, which is unconventional, because most sellers are most relaxed during the early phases of a sales campaign. This is also true in government or public sales where an acquisition's outcome can be informally determined long before the bid and proposal phase—the time when conventionally thinking sellers are busiest.

TIMING AND THE ELEMENT OF SURPRISE

The upfront speed and back-end surprise are key elements of the *Indirect* strategy. As stated earlier, some sellers will hold back on the Unexpected Value until a very specific and crucial point in time. For example, you are running two separate sales campaigns simultaneously for our ATM sales opportunity: one based on expected value to the Facilities Department and the other based on Unexpected Value to the retail banking business unit.

This requires that you align quickly with the Situational Power Base. You need to Milestone Stack to observe that the retail banking Fox will likely become the Situational Fox and that he will direct the Facilities Department Power Base. While gathering this type of insight early in a sales campaign depends on the flurry of activity associated with Stacking, this upfront speed enables you to achieve the element of back-end surprise for two reasons:

1. The unexpected potential value that moves you high up on the Sales Value Chain is intangible and therefore invisible to your competition.
2. Your competition is likely to believe that you are implementing a *Direct* strategy. His Supporters will inform him that you have been calling on the Facilities Department and haven't made a stronger case for lower price and increased uptime. When your apparent *Direct* approach appears weak, as it almost always will, your competitor may develop a false sense of security that causes him to become overconfident. He may therefore underestimate you as a threat and perhaps even reduce his customer responsiveness. He cannot see what is coming.

So, what exactly *is* coming?

When the sales cycle peaks, you will pull the rug out from beneath your competitor at the 11th hour.

Unlike the *Direct* strategy, which always favors closing as early as possible, you want the sales cycle to peak as late as possible in this scenario, for two reasons:

1. You will catch your competitor off guard by using the element of surprise. He may not even understand the world that exists high up on the Sales Value Chain and probably won't have many executive relationships to provide support. Still, you will get some kind of a response. It might be an attempt to emulate the Unexpected Value you provide; sometimes your competitor may even pull it off if time permits.

   You can protect yourself by doing everything possible to help peak the sales situation as late in the sales cycle as possible. This prevents your competitor from having the time needed to catch up and counter your approach. In the ATM example, he might announce that his product is going to have a similar revenue-generating feature. In that event, you would, essentially, be deploying a *Direct* strategy. It could still be successful, but why take the risk?

2. Sellers rarely launch into sales cycles as early as they would like. It's clearly optimal to be working with the customer long before an acquisition goes out for bid. And sometimes that is the case, particularly when Stage IV Customer Advisors create demand for a solution that then becomes the focus of a prewired RFP. However, it usually takes sellers time to align with the Situational Power Base and move up the Sales Value Chain. The longer it takes for the sales situation to peak, the more time you have to put all the pieces in place to change the ground rules, still recognizing the need for "upfront speed" as discussed earlier.

THE *INDIRECT* STRATEGY STATEMENT

The key elements to the *Indirect* strategy statement include:

- The class of strategy
- The critical customer business focus of the strategy, such as unexpected customer value

- The critical political focus of the strategy, for example, on a Fox's specific Personal Motivator
- Unexpected or discounted competitor vulnerability, such as an installed supplier's overconfidence or a weakness in solution capability as it relates to providing value higher up on the Sales Value Chain
- Early achievement of the Prime Objective by using Milestone Stacking
- Timing that ensures the element of surprise and the competition's inability to respond effectively

When these elements are combined, again, you have not only a strategy statement but a theme for the entire sales campaign. All activities and new developments are then judged against that theme. An example of such an *Indirect* strategy statement, utilizing our ATM sales scenario, is the following.

Our *Indirect* strategy is to change the ground rules from uptime and price to providing the Unexpected Value of revenue generation to advance the corporation's growth goal and the retail banking Fox's Personal Motivator of winning the current Power Struggle with commercial lending, by achieving our Prime Objective by July 9.

A general template to assist you with this consists of the tool in Figure 14.4.

Figure 14.4
***Indirect* Strategy Statement Template**

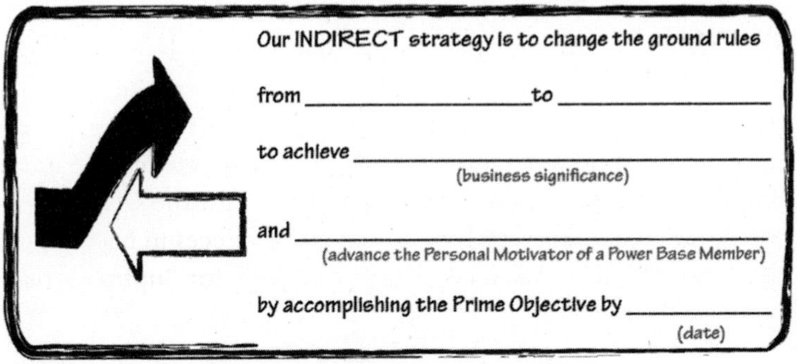

Our INDIRECT strategy is to change the ground rules

from _____ to _____

to achieve _____
            (business significance)

and _____
    (advance the Personal Motivator of a Power Base Member)

by accomplishing the Prime Objective by _____
                                        (date)

CONCLUSION

The *Indirect* strategy is the technologically advanced *steel* sword of your sales campaign. Its strength symbolizes unconventional thinking and the power of the intangibles—politics, potential unexpected customer value, and mind-set—all leveraged by the right strategy. Still, there will be occasions when you rule out the *Direct* approach and can find no satisfactory way to change the ground rules to go *Indirect*. When that happens, it's time to consider yet another approach to winning, so on we go to the *Divisional* strategy.

CHAPTER 15

THE DIVISIONAL STRATEGY

PEACEFUL COEXISTENCE

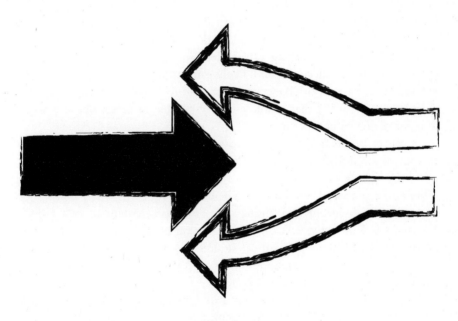

If the enemy's forces are united, separate them.

—Sun Tzu

The divide and conquer approach to winning battles is well documented throughout military history. The opposition is also being divided in selling; although not physically, the business being pursued is being split among two suppliers.

Sellers use the Divisional strategy to complement their competitor, to secure a part of the business, to build from in the future.

The *Divisional* approach is a cousin of the *Direct* strategy; in fact, someone viewing its application from a tactical perspective might not even be able to tell them apart. But the intent behind the *Divisional* strategy is quite different from that of a *Direct* approach.

You go *Divisional* when you can't overpower the competition and take all the available business. A seller will realize this after running a Competitive Differentiation Analysis and comparing Attack and Defend points. Recall also that your Support Base must be sufficient enough to facilitate whatever class of strategy you wish to deploy. If you don't have the relative superiority to go *Direct* or change the ground rules with an *Indirect* approach, you must scale back your aspirations and work to secure at least a piece of the business. Think of it as taking a beachhead in order to have a place within the account. If you succeed, you'll likely gain an opportunity to expand and strengthen your Support Base while you figure out how to move up the Sales Value Chain. At that point, you may be able to break out and more directly challenge competitors.

However, reducing the scope of your solution won't make life any easier. It is much more manageable for a customer to work with one supplier who provides a total solution than it is to work with multiple companies, each of which offers a part of the solution. The exception occurs when a customer is seeking to divide up the business for risk management or cost reduction reasons. But if that isn't the case, then you need to demonstrate to the customer's satisfaction that you can address a specific application in a way that is far superior to your competition's approach. And that doesn't mean simply having more features and benefits.

You will have to show some kind of Unexpected Value to offset any compatibility, financial, or intellectual property issues associated with coexisting with the competitor. So it's still crucial to move up the Sales Value Chain, because it will help you align with the Situational Fox or Enterprise Power Base members. Competitors don't tolerate one another very well, much less want to work together. They usually do this only when customers require it—and that means Fox involvement!

PEACEFUL COEXISTENCE

Two words characterize what it takes for a *Divisional* strategy to succeed: *peaceful coexistence*. The question, however, is how this actually comes to be.

What could possibly prompt two parties who inherently distrust each other to work together? When the concept was first introduced, it primarily involved post–World War II Russia, a communist nation, and the United States, a democratic nation, joining forces. In essence, the Soviet Union wanted to improve relations with the West and offset the notion that Russia's goal was world revolution. But what does that have to do with selling?

Two factors drove world acceptance of this new concept: risk and reward. The risk part for these two nations was easy to understand: peaceful coexistence would reduce the tension between them; that would in turn reduce the risk of mistakes and bad judgment that could potentially trigger a nuclear war. On the reward side, the Russians aimed to defeat the West with a focus on economics, because they believed that socialism would ultimately triumph over capitalism. So the reward for them was the ability to spread socialism more quickly, which is why they formed the World Peace Council in 1949.

These same two factors apply to the deployment of the *Divisional* strategy. The risk motivation for a competitor exists when they feel that their solution to a customer's requirements might fail and put future business in jeopardy. This will compel them to run a risk assessment on you. If they believe that you could be a future threat by working a migration path into their installed base, they will fight you at every turn and look for a different partner to recommend to the customer. But if they don't see such intent or capability, they will likely be more responsive. Therefore, *it is absolutely key that you not make your competitor aware of your intent to expand your base in the account.*

The competitor's reward is to maintain account control and be able to position his or her company as a total solution provider with you as subordinate to them. Even if you do have the intent to expand, the competitor will have the better and stronger executive relationships that will assist him or her in containing you.

This, of course, is a more traditional approach—and what our data tells us that you can likely expect. On the other hand, the long-term outcome may be very different if you think and operate like a Stage IV Customer Advisor who knows how to leverage the intangibles. By the time the competition realizes that you have moved up the Sales Value Chain and aligned with the Power Base, that seller will likely have been displaced from the account or relegated to a small amount of business. Although it is often difficult for them to see the intangibles, it is not difficult to see the result of being outsold.

THE OVERCONFIDENT SUPPLIER

Some established suppliers within accounts essentially "fall asleep" from time to time. This usually occurs when a seller thinks that he or she owns an account and develops a false sense of confidence and security. These sellers may neglect the account to such a point that the customer doesn't feel that they are committed to supporting them—and that they might be taking their business for granted. There could even be enough minor issues to prompt the customer individuals to forget all the good work that the seller has done, thereby shifting their focus to the difficulties. However, sellers often miss this, for a couple of reasons:

1. They may feel that the customer is operationally locked in and unable to switch suppliers for whatever reason.
2. Many tend to hear what they want to hear and therefore become unknowingly insensitive to developing problems.

Whatever the cause, this condition provides an opportunity for a competitor to challenge the installed base. Let's say that you are that competitor and that the installed base consists of high-speed, high-capacity core routers resident within a telecommunications company or service provider. At the same time that the installed supplier is becoming a bit complacent, a new need for smarter edge routers emerges. Normally, this would be a shoo-in for the incumbent. But things could be different this time.

You launch your campaign with an intel-gathering effort that suggests the following:

- You have an advantage over the installed supplier in terms of your intelligent edge router ability to manage different types of traffic. However, this advantage on its own is not significant enough to give you the relative superiority necessary to win the business.
- There does not appear to be any opportunity to move up the Sales Value Chain and provide the customer with Unexpected Value at this time.
- Fortunately, you have been able to connect with an Emerging Fox who is *not* aligned with your competitor. Furthermore, this individual's Personal Motivator is to move up in the organization, which means that he is sensitive to recognition from others. Your Fox Hunting also suggests that he has a relationship with the Enterprise Fox. This is important because the Situational Fox *does* have a Supporter relationship with the incumbent.
- You've confirmed that the installed supplier is definitely overconfident and has been less than responsive for some months as far as the customer is concerned.

These observations help you form a picture of the sales campaign. First, you'll need to keep the sales cycle short, because you don't want to give the incumbent time to correct the performance issues. Although you currently have an advantage there, the real play is to provide the customer with value—not from your company, but from the incumbent's company. As ironic as it sounds, the majority of the value that you will provide will be as a catalyst that forces the competition to clean up its act. The Emerging Fox will receive the credit when you do this, thus advancing his Personal Motivator. All this is possible because your competitor is predictable, desensitized to competitive threat, and particularly vulnerable to the unconventional thinking that will enable you to create the element of surprise.

So, how might all this unfold? You leverage your relationship with the Emerging Fox to not only drive the edge router performance advantage but also gain access to business leads in departments outside of Information Technology (IT). You then focus on the business value associated with this advantage while simultaneously letting them know that they aren't receiving sufficient service and support in the larger core router installations. However, you never disparage the competition. You just emphasize the business importance of the support that you will provide, recognizing that the Emerging Fox will do the rest—and with a lot more credibility and impact than if you attempted it. Your job is simply to set the stage.

It won't be long before the pieces to the sales campaign, and specifically your *Divisional* strategy, take shape. You use Milestone Stacking to coordinate efforts to meet business leads who can influence IT and begin to advance the Emerging Fox's Personal Motivator. You also trap the competitor by informally educating the Emerging Fox about the incumbent's unresponsiveness to the account—again, not by speaking ill of that company, but by stressing how *your* company operates.

Sooner or later, the incumbent will hear alarm bells when he realizes you're gaining traction. This is where the sales situation gets interesting. Unbeknown to the incumbent, you have already achieved your Prime Objective: to develop the Emerging Fox into a Supporter. Your competition thinks that he is in trouble because of the poor support and the performance issue on the edge routers; although these are factors, the *real* problem is that he is being outsold *politically*.

You achieved a decisive advantage over the competition that gave you relative superiority the moment that the Emerging Fox became a Supporter. Yes, the incumbent can improve service and support, or bring in the Chief Executive Officer (CEO) to put forth company commitments;

however, the incumbent cannot justify his company's actions. At this point, they're claiming to want to do the right things, but for the wrong reasons. They are not enhancing their support of the account because they are committed to the customer's success, but because you have a figurative gun to their head.

The Emerging Fox understands this (with your help) and is prepared to argue that her company should not continue to depend on a supplier who doesn't have its best interests at heart. In this respect, you are basically outcaring your competition. The result is decisive, as you secure the order for the edge router business and establish a foothold from which to grow.

THE DIVISIONAL STRATEGY STATEMENT

The key elements to a *Divisional* strategy statement include:

- The class of strategy
- Your solution focus (and its business significance) that will complement the competition in terms of moving up the Sales Value Chain
- The critical political focus of the strategy, such as on a Fox's specific Personal Motivator
- Unexpected or discounted competitor vulnerability, such as an installed supplier's overconfidence or a weakness in solution capability as it relates to providing value higher up on the Sales Value Chain
- Early achievement of the Prime Objective by using Milestone Stacking

Combining these elements once again allows you to develop a theme for the entire sales campaign against which you can assess all future activities and new developments. An example of such a *Divisional* strategy statement is the following:

> Our *Divisional* strategy is to focus on the edge router business, advancing the corporation's IT direction of moving to a smart edge and fast core, while advancing the Emerging Fox's Personal Motivator of upward mobility by leveraging the competition's overconfidence, along with the achievement of our Prime Objective by July 9.

A general template to assist you with this consists of the tool in Figure 15.1.

Figure 15.1
Divisional **Strategy Statement Template**

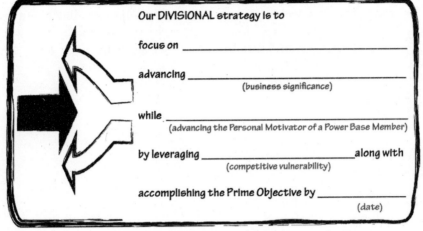

Our DIVISIONAL strategy is to

focus on _____

advancing _____
               (business significance)

while _____
        (advancing the Personal Motivator of a Power Base Member)

by leveraging _____ along with
                (competitive vulnerability)

accomplishing the Prime Objective by _____
                                        (date)

CONCLUSION

Again, sales strategy is the intellectual sword of your sales campaign. But now, we are not going to talk about the metallurgy of the sword. Instead, we look at a new type of sword that is based on the fighting environment.

During the days of feudal Japan, the samurai would carry traditional long swords, one of which was called the katana. Strong and resilient with a sharp and durable edge, it was an amazingly effective weapon. But in close quarters, its length actually diminished its efficacy. The samurai needed an alternative in these situations—as it is with a seller who judges that the selling environment is not conducive to a *Direct* or *Indirect* strategy.

The samurai solution to this problem was to carry a complement: the short wakizashi sword. As a samurai entered a house, for example, he would take off his katana and leave it at the door. But the short sword would remain securely with him. It was less powerful, but it was correctly sized to the conditions, just as the *Divisional* strategy can be in certain sales campaigns. Having said that, the samurai were master warriors with or without weapons—they always had options. And even when no class of strategy appears applicable, so do you.

- You could *walk away* from the opportunity. That doesn't sound very good to most sellers, and it sounds even worse to sales managers, but there are times when you simply shouldn't compete because your cost of sales will be too high and your win potential is too low.

- A second option is to appear to compete in order to raise the price of victory for the competition and to maintain a presence in the account should circumstances change.
- Third, you could attempt to slow down the customer's buying process, buying you enough time to gather the strength required to win the business with an *Indirect* strategy. This *Containment* approach is the focus of our next chapter.

CHAPTER 16

THE CONTAINMENT STRATEGY

TRANSITION BACK TO INDIRECT

Though the enemy be stronger in numbers, we may prevent him from fighting.

—Sun Tzu

If you are *not* able to win the business with a *Direct, Indirect,* or *Divisional* approach, you should consider the *Containment* strategy. Its purpose is to delay the customer's decision, therefore buying you enough time to gather strength and win the business with an *Indirect* approach. The two strategies work seamlessly in tandem with each other.

Even a short delay before a sales situation peaks can cause a disproportionate impact on all the competitors. For example, your competitor will presumably be working hard to synchronize her sales strategy to that point when the customer is ready, willing, and able to make a purchase decision. At that point, every day that goes by without closing the deal represents a geometric increase in her vulnerability. Other competitors may improve their solution during this time, possibly providing a lower price and preferred business terms. Changes in the customer environment, such as a shift in the Situational Power Base, a reallocation of budget, or a restructuring of the organization, may occur, thus destabilizing *everyone's* sales campaign.

The challenge, however, is not delaying the customer evaluation for several days or a week, because this will likely assist the customer by referencing some future event or new information that will help him with his evaluation. The real challenge is figuring out what to do with the time you now have. But before we dive into that, let's be clear as to how you can actually delay a decision.

As you know from Chapter 13, three customer states must be present for a sales situation to peak and for a close condition to exist. The customer must be ready, willing, and able to make a decision, having effectively evaluated all the potential suppliers.

When you implement a *Containment* strategy, you are eliminating the customer's *ready* state to make a decision.

Knowing that you lack the relative superiority to win a sales situation that is about to peak, you introduce new insight that the customer will want to include as part of the evaluation process, thus slowing it down until the insight can be gained. For example, imagine that you've arranged a meeting between the customer and a recognized industry leader, perhaps someone like your Chief Executive Officer (CEO) or Vice President (VP) of Research and Development. You might explain to the customer that your CEO would like to meet with him to put forth a corporate commitment to the success of your solution. If the competition then tries to close the deal before this has occurred, the customer might say, "We do plan to make a decision shortly, as we are just completing our evaluation." If the customer individual is a Competitor Supporter or Ally, he or she may go further and explain the reason for the delay; however, it is unlikely to alter the situation. Again, this will be only a few days, not weeks; you cannot eliminate the ready state for very long. This brings us back to the point of what to do with the time you now have.

It makes sense to implement a *Containment* strategy when you are in second place and have miscalculated somewhere during the sales campaign. Perhaps the person you thought to be the Fox turned out, on further investigation, to not even be a member of the Situational Power Base. Mistakes like this happen, because sales is a management science and not an exact science. You might have misread certain customer requirements or you might not have made your way high up enough on the Sales Value Chain. Whatever the reason, there needs to be a specific issue—of which you are aware—that has put you in second place and is the problem you are buying time to address.

Your sales manager might want to know why you weren't aware of it sooner; however, a peaking sales situation gives you visibility into what is going on far more clearly than earlier in the sales cycle. Having said that, it's not enough to just fix the problem. You need to gather some new piece of information, one that would have likely influenced the customer's support for you if he or she had known about it earlier. We refer to this as a *face-saver*.

If a customer individual has voiced support for your competition, that person needs a legitimate reason for shifting positions. Without such a reason, it will look like he or she is flip-flopping indecisively, damaging his or her credibility. So if you caused a delay in the customer decision by setting up a meeting with your CEO, for example, *your executive must do two things: fix the compete problem and provide a face-saver for those who have supported your competition.*

The best way to accomplish this is to change the ground rules with an *Indirect* sales strategy. If the CEO can move your solution higher up on the Sales Value Chain in a manner that advances the Situational Fox's Personal Motivator, you will likely pull the rug out from under the competition, while enabling customer individuals to save face and support you. This is a lot to accomplish, so it's best to think of it as Milestone Stacking with the CEO doing the heavy lifting.

There are specific times and circumstances when it makes sense to use a *Containment* approach, and there are times when it does not. Delaying a customer decision and *hoping* that circumstances will change is not a great use of time. And you never want to involve your senior management unless you understand exactly what you are doing. Otherwise, you risk creating some negative high-level exposure for yourself.

The key is to use a *Containment* approach only when you really need it—and one way you'll know is if you've exhausted every possibility to effectively employ one of the other three classes of strategy. We recommend something that we call a Red Cell exercise to accomplish this.

THE RED CELL EXERCISE

Red Cell is a term that was created in 1984 by Richard Marcinko, US Navy commander of the elite counterterrorist unit SEAL Team Six. His mission was to test US naval bases' security by launching mock attacks and simulating terrorists to discover whether any vulnerability existed. Although this is clearly quite different from a sales environment, it can be both revealing and productive to put yourself in the "enemy's," or the competition's, shoes. However, this is solely the domain of those Stage III and IV sellers who possess the kind of offensive mind-set we presented earlier.

You can conduct a Red Cell exercise by introducing people who are new to the sales situation to the opportunity that you're pursuing. It is helpful if they know the account, but if they don't, you can compensate to some degree with your briefing, which is where you begin the exercise.

1. **Brief the team on the customer.** You provide the participants or team with a *customer intel package* that familiarizes them with the customer's industry, market position, and business in terms of structure, historical performance, vision, direction, priorities, competition, and any other relevant information. You share with them the insight gained from your research, observations, and questions.

2. **Present your *Compete Plan* to win.** You educate participants on the sales opportunity, account, competition, and your Compete Strategy. This Compete Plan consists of a few short pages composed of information on:

   • **Political Advantage:** your *Support Base Map,* the Situational Power Base, the Situational Fox (and his or her Personal Motivator), and competitive contacts

   • **Unexpected Value:** where you reside on the *Sales Value Chain,* along with your associated *Value Statement* and *Value Proposition*

   • **Competitive Differentiation:** your *Competitive Differentiation Analysis*

   • **Strategy:** your *Strategy Statement*

3. **Simulate your competitor.** You then assume the role of the competitor with one of the participants leading the role-play by thinking and acting like the competitor. The more that person knows about the specific competitor, the better. This is why it's best to gather competitive intel before the exercise begins.

   The team simulates the competition by determining how they will defeat you. Specifically, they begin with a Competitive Differentiation Analysis and focus heavily on the Attack and Defend boxes. The team takes about an hour to construct a competitive counteroffensive, which they'll express as a version of one of the four strategy classes. They will also identify their sales objective, along with the Prime Objective, identifying how and when they expect to achieve relative superiority. Again, all of this is from your competitor's point of view.

4. **Catalog areas of vulnerability.** When you've completed the exercise, everyone reverts to a role on your team to catalog areas of vulnerability and reconstruct a Competitive Differentiation Analysis that reflects what has been learned.

From there, you formulate a new or enhanced Compete Strategy. However, you've now tested it and therefore you have greatly enhanced insight into the sales situation. This insight will enable you to prepare for the implementation of a *Containment* strategy should you need it. We recommend completing a Red Cell exercise for all sales campaigns that are highly competitive and important. Figure 16.1 summarizes this process.

Figure 16.1
The Red Cell Exercise

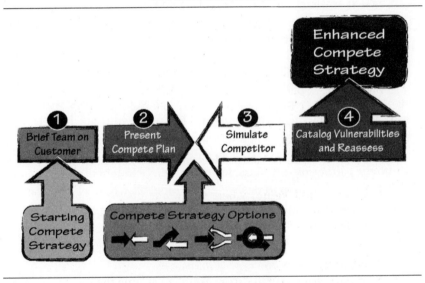

Now, let's look at examples wherein deploying a *Containment* strategy naturally transitions to an *Indirect* approach at the 11th hour.

INTRODUCING A NEW PRODUCT ROAD MAP OR INDUSTRY EXPERTISE

A good place to start is to arrange a meeting with someone of stature from your company whom the customer will perceive as bringing new insight worthy of knowing before they make a decision. This person should be a recognized industry leader or expert; an ideal candidate is the executive on point for your product's future vision. If you know that your company is about to release a new product that will exceed the customer's buying criteria and move you up on the Sales Value Chain, you will likely be able to delay the sales situation by arranging a meeting with such a person.

You must then use this meeting to address whatever compete problem exists. Perhaps it is a political alignment issue, or maybe an Opponent is creating difficulty for you. Your business terms or pricing may be an issue. You must address your disadvantage during the delay period, thereby *enabling you to repackage your solution and implement an Indirect strategy.* Whenever you think about *Containment,* think about repackaging your solution and moving north in the account. This is not only the core to this strategy but the bridge to an *Indirect* approach and winning the business.

INTRODUCING A NEW PARTNER TO BROADEN THE SOLUTION

How do you enhance your solution and move up the Sales Value Chain when you have exhausted what your company has to offer? One answer is to partner with another company; together, you can strengthen or broaden your solution. This is usually a possibility when you can work with niche players who complement your solution. However, you will have to take responsibility for the complete solution in order to make this work.

Operationally, the process is one of entering into an agreement in principle with the partner, usually in the form of a memorandum of understanding (MOU). You'll then have to determine the probable nature of this relationship; will they be subordinate, an equal partner, or should you form a joint venture? Whatever the arrangement, *the key is to buy time, move up on the Sales Value Chain, and align with the Power Base in order to change the ground rules.*

THE CONTAINMENT STRATEGY STATEMENT

The key elements in a *Containment* strategy statement include:

- The class of strategy
- Your approach to delaying the decision and making certain that the customer *perceives value in doing so.* A clever but worthless delaying tactic will serve only to annoy the customer and damage your credibility. You have to contribute to the evaluation process in real terms. And remember, you can take only a short time, such as a few days or a week. This might not be long; however, its impact on competitors is, again, disproportionate to the amount of time.
- Which compete issues you will address during the delay

- How you will move up the Sales Value Chain and improve your political alignment
- How you will smoothly bridge from the *Containment* approach to the *Indirect* strategy—complete with a face-saver. Stay on the offensive, which reflects driving ambition tempered by humility. Remember, your mission is not to delay the decision, but to win the business.

Combining these elements provides you with both a strategy statement and specific direction to turning around a competitive sales situation. As with the other strategies, you can then judge all activities and new developments against this mission.

An example of such a *Containment* strategy statement is the following:

Our *Containment* strategy is to delay the decision by bringing in our VP of R&D to confidentially brief the Situational Fox on our new capabilities in order to address their perception that our product does not integrate with their installed base. We will do this while moving up the Sales Value Chain, by accelerating the customer's new cost reduction initiatives and improving our political alignment by advancing the Fox's Personal Motivator of balanced lifestyle, thus changing the ground rules from the existing criteria to providing unexpected cost savings.

Figure 16.2 shows the template for a *Containment* strategy statement.

Figure 16.2
***Containment* Strategy Statement Template**

Our CONTAINMENT strategy is to delay the decision

by _____
                    (approach)

in order to address_____
                          (compete issues and solutions)

while moving up the Sales Value Chain by_____
                                              (approach)

and improving our political alignment by_____
                                              (approach)

and thus change the ground rules from the existing criteria

to_____
        (new criteria)

ONE LAST POINT ABOUT THE CONTAINMENT STRATEGY

We have said many times that strategy is the intellectual sword of your sales campaign, because strategy is a confrontation of competing minds driven by situational awareness and wisdom. It might be two opposing generals, sellers, politicians, employees, or any other two people engaged in a zero-sum conflict. For this reason, Stage III and IV sellers think through how they will win early in a sales campaign—particularly when they need an asymmetric advantage. If things don't work out, they keep thinking, perhaps utilizing the *Containment* strategy. But there is one last important nuance to make tangible—and that is *emotion*. We turn to an example from history to show this point.

In April 1612 on an island in Japan, two famous swordsmen and undefeated masters named Miyamoto Musashi and Sasaki Kojiro were to fight to the death.[1] These men were very much opposites. Kojiro had social position, power, wealth, and a strong following, whereas Musashi had no interest in such things. Kojiro depended on fighting technique and his weapon for success, while Musashi focused more on his powers of observation and intuition. He considered technique and weapons to be important, but he counted on the intangible to win—specifically, the power of his mind. Kojiro also had an advantage. His sword was unusually long and extremely well made; he was thus able to overpower other swordsmen who used the more traditional shorter sword. When the time to compete came, Kojiro had been in place and ready for some time. However, Musashi was not there.

After a long and frustrating wait, Musashi's boat finally arrived. When he climbed out, he was carrying a wooden sword that he had fashioned out of one of the boat's oars. Kojiro was outraged and lost control of his emotions for the first time. Arriving late and using a wooden sword was an unacceptable insult. However, this was all part of Musashi's plan. Kojiro's brilliant technique diminished as his anger grew, enabling Musashi to defeat him with nothing more than his wooden sword.

All odds were against Musashi, just as it is with a seller who is behind in the 11th hour of a peaking sales situation. But with time and strategy, Musashi influenced and leveraged his opponent's *emotions*. Such is the case in a peaking sales opportunity where there is no room for mistakes and emotions run high. Many sellers become predictable at these times and deal poorly with adversity. It is because of this emotional environment that you can

---

[1] For more information, read *The Lone Samurai: The Life of Miyamoto Musashi,* by William Scott Wilson (Tokyo: Kodansha International Ltd., 2004).

reverse purchase decisions if you prepare and move strategically, with "careful hurry." The *Containment* approach exists for this purpose.

CONCLUSION

Musashi was one of the greatest samurai ever. He was the real deal—the complete package. Unlike other swordsmen, he took a holistic approach to competition that always incorporated unconventional thinking to leverage his skills, resources, and timing, while exploiting his opponent's unexpected vulnerability. He was a master of the intangibles.

In today's selling, this translates into the ability to apply unconventional thinking to provide customers with Unexpected Value, while identifying and professionally exploiting unexpected competitor vulnerability.

It has been 400 years since Musashi stood on that island to fight Kojiro. And the mastery of competition still rests with the intangibles.

Helping Others Elevate the Sales Profession

Lead me, follow me, or get out of my way.

—General Patton

As we introduced at the beginning of this book, 80 percent of sellers are at a Stage I and II level of proficiency. Not surprisingly, most company's sales infrastructure is geared to those levels. They focus on the tangible sources of competitive advantage and not on the intangible sources of relative superiority—politics, Unexpected Value, and strategy. Although many of you have the internal motivation and drive to excel to Stage III or IV without your company's support, you will move more easily and quickly with it.

With this gap between Stage III and IV selling and Stage I and II company infrastructure in mind, we encourage you to share this message with your sales manager to help yourself and other sellers in your company. Explain that an updated company infrastructure will produce a number of opportunities for new business. Namely:

- **Consistently Higher Win Rates:** Win rates in most industries are in the neighborhood of 30 percent as a result of heavy Stage II selling. Basically, and on average, 3 out of 10 deals are won. But those 3 deals must carry the cost of sales for all 10, which also impacts margins. Even a small increase in win rate for the right types of deals can produce a disproportionate increase in revenue.
- **Unexpected Increase in Customer Satisfaction:** Executive-level customer satisfaction scores tend to be lower for Stage II seller

installations, which confuses your company image with customer executives and reduces future competitiveness in terms of repeat business. This is all about executive customer loyalty and the opportunity to improve it.

- **Increased Wallet Share:** The best way to take the lion's share of business within major accounts is with a Stage IV Customer Advisor at the helm. These sellers not only pursue individual opportunities but build a plan to effectively leverage customer politics, value, and strategy to take the majority of the business. Scaling up the number of Customer Advisors takes market share from competitors, one major account at a time.

Aligning the company's sales support infrastructure with all the stages of selling has the potential to create significant short- and long-term business impact. To affect this alignment, however, requires a bit of nontraditional thinking and an understanding of how sellers develop. When sellers learn new and innovative sales concepts, ideas, and techniques, they go through four phases of development:

1. *Awareness of the New Thinking:* Simply knowing that specific techniques exist and what they consist of in terms of intent.
2. *Understanding:* Knowing how to operationalize the new techniques; what they are, how they work, when to use them, and what to expect for results.
3. *Skill Development:* Having the ability to actually implement what has been learned, which best occurs when sellers apply and adapt what has been learned to their specific selling environment (we refer to this as contextual learning).
4. *Belief:* Seeing the results and knowing how the techniques and new thinking contributed to those results. If sellers don't believe in something, they will not continue with it. Conversely, when they try something new and it works, they are often enthusiastic and supportive.

Sometimes, organizations unintentionally try to achieve results through the awareness and understanding phases of learning, without a detailed bridge to the skill development and "belief" phases that are required to create powerful and sustainable results. This common Stage I and II *training* approach looks a lot like what you see in Figure E.1.

Figure E.1
Stage I and II Traditional Training Approach

Source: Sydney Harris, ScienceCartoonsPlus.com. Used with permission.

So what is missing? What is the miracle? We suggest you engage in a discussion with your sales manager that looks at selling as a management science, bringing to life the intangibles. All too often, the array of skill-based training programs that companies offer, although helpful, lack *relevance* in terms of providing customers with Unexpected Value while advancing sellers to relative superiority. This relevance is added in a Level 1 sales infra-structure that connects skills to managing politics, value, and strategy within accounts.

LEVEL 1: ESTABLISHING RELEVANCE

Rather than training sellers on isolated skills such as probing, handling objections, generating proposals, giving presentations, and so on, a Stage III and IV infrastructure integrates these skills with the intangibles. It threads all the appropriate skills together to produce nontraditional sources of relative superiority for sellers. The result is a cohesive, well-integrated curriculum where all the skills work in concert, geometrically increasing win rates and the value provided to customers.

Now that the training is centered on the customer and competition, the next step is to help sellers learn to implement what has been taught, which brings us to the Level 2 sales infrastructure.

LEVEL 2: DRIVING ADOPTION

The best way to *learn* is to *do!* Adoption is accomplished through sales man-agement coaching in the field, specifically by conducting deal reviews that encourage and support sellers as they adapt and apply sales-relevant skills. In addition, many sales managers will link the application of new skills to pipeline management and sales forecasting.

In this way, for example, the pipeline not only tells you how a sales situation is progressing, in terms of activities, but also indicates whether you are winning or losing. So, within a region or district, the skills become locally institutionalized. Having said that, the effectiveness of a Level 2 sales infrastructure will vary as sales managers vary. Having established proof of concept in two or three regions, the next step is to link the application of key sales skills to companywide sales practices. This brings you to Level 3 of the sales infrastructure.

LEVEL 3: CREATING SUSTAINABLE IMPACT

It is at this level that executives start infusing these integrated skills through-out the organization. Here are just a few of the best practices we've seen.

Sales Process

- *Pipeline Management:* Advancing from one phase of the pipeline to another requires that certain compete activities take place. For example, as a gating requirement, the Fox would need to be identified before you enter the proposal stage.
- *Customer Relationship Management (CRM):* Opportunity and account plans are automated to make the skills easier to implement and manage. Because these tools produce insight for the seller, the traditional use of the CRM may increase as well.

Marketing

- *Value Statements:* The marketing team catalogs industry-specific expressions of value to assist sellers in moving up the Sales Value Chain.
- *Competitive Intelligence:* Here, example Competitive Differentiation Analysis matrixes are produced for primary competitors to assist sellers in formulating a Compete Strategy for specific deals.

Human Resources (HR)

- *Compensation:* The HR team links compensation to key selling behaviors in order to motivate and recognize Stage III and IV success.
- *Hiring:* Here, the required core competencies that drive the right behaviors are integrated with the recruiting and selection process to better identify, hire, and retain Stage III and IV sellers.

Finance

- *Bid and Proposal Funding:* The finance and sales management teams work together to establish opportunity qualification criteria to justify the cost of a sales pursuit in order to ensure the right amount of focus on the right deals.

THREE-LEVEL SALES PERFORMANCE INFRASTRUCTURE

The result is a company infrastructure that doesn't end with isolated sales training, but rather a three-level sales performance system that advances sellers to relevance with strong adoption that becomes sustainable. This approach is summarized in Figure E.2.

Figure E.2
Three-Level Sales Performance System

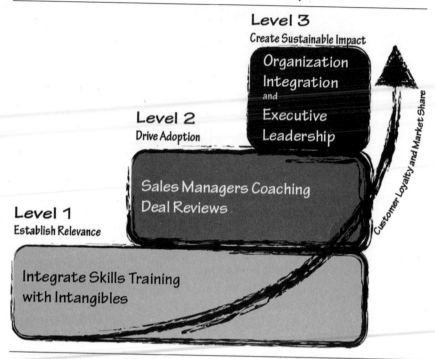

This system first elevates sellers to become Customer Advisors. Then it scales up their number in a sustainable manner that produces an enterprise asset for the company. This is an asset that builds on the product, technology, service levels, and the company's reputation to provide unprecedented customer value and high win rates. An asset that is tangible, but that stems from the intangibles!

CONCLUSION

As a Customer Advisor, or someone with the potential to become one, you have a voice and a responsibility. If you can see your future success, you can see the kind of support system required to assist you and others, as we have introduced with the three-level sales performance system. Use this book to quickly reach your potential, but then help others. Many sellers will not make it to Stage IV on their own. They have ability and commitment, but will need help. As a high performer, your voice will be heard.

Be the spark within your company to elevate the sales profession to that of a management science, providing Unexpected Value to your customers, beyond product, price, and brand, so that everybody wins—your customer, your company, you, and, over time, the selling profession.

INDEX

LIST OF FIGURES

LIST OF FIGURES (*CONTINUED*)